MW01065584

Blueprint
21

Blueprint 21

Presbyterians in the Post-Denominational Era

ROBERT THORNTON HENDERSON

PROVIDENCE HOUSE PUBLISHERS
Franklin, Tennessee

Copyright 2000 by Robert Thornton Henderson

All rights reserved. Written permission must be secured from the publisher to use or reproduce any part of this book, except for brief quotations in critical reviews or articles.

Printed in the United States of America

04   03   02   01   00   1   2   3   4   5

Library of Congress Catalog Card Number: 00-107585

ISBN: 1-57736-203-9

Cover design by Gary Bozeman

PROVIDENCE HOUSE PUBLISHERS
238 Seaboard Lane • Franklin, Tennessee 37067
800-321-5692
www.providencehouse.com

To

Generation X and Generation Y

(the Millennial Generation)

among whom I anticipate the next

great awakening by the Holy Spirit.

Contents

Preface & Acknowledgments

MY READERS ARE DUE SOME EXPLANATION, SOME *APOLOGIA*, FOR this outrageous book. First to say that I wrote this in 1996 for myself, never really thinking that anyone would ever be interested in such an excursion into the future. I wondered what it would look like in 2020 given the things that were already obvious. But in conversations with others who were looking at the same fluid ecclesiastical scene in the Presbyterian family, and sharing with them my own writings on this, more and more asked for copies of what I was writing. It is, in obvious ways, a very personal sojourn, as is evidenced in the lament in chapter 5.

My pilgrimage as a pastor-teacher in the Presbyterian Church began with many years of ministry to university students. I suppose it was they who provoked me into thinking about current and future cultural issues. One of my early mentors encouraged me to pray for the gift of the "men of Issachar" (1 Chron. 12:32) who saw the issues of the times to give Israel guidance. However it happened, I tend to think into the future. I tend to read others who venture into this risky discipline of futurizing. There is really nothing original in this book. I have been nurtured by the writings of more gifted Issachar-ites such as Robert Wuthnow, Leith Anderson, Leonard Sweet, Howard Snyder, Tom Sine, Russell Chandler, Albert Borgman, and many others. I am grateful to them for their provocations into an altogether new cultural context.

I am unapologetic in my conviction that the day of denominations *as we have known them* is now past. In a conversation with one of our church history faculty in a Presbyterian seminary, I asked: How long do you give denominations? His response: "They are done, finished. They no longer register on the scope." Very few persons presently join churches because of their denominational label. The church as a missional community, however, will always need some framework, some *wineskin* in which to operate, but the form must be flexible and versatile to the mission.

I am also unapologetic that the reason for which our particular Presbyterian part of the family of God exists is not that we have a *Presbyterian* form of government, but that we have a particular stance within the larger church known as the *Reformed* tradition. This is our gift to the larger family of God (cf. chapter 2 of the *Book of Order*). But then I must apologize to my friends who are formally trained in Reformed theology, since they may not recognize my take (or spin) on Reformed thinking! But I am a pastoral pragmatist, and I offer my thinking on a "Reformed Household for Generation X" as a challenge. I want the glory of the Creator God who "creates, sustains, rules, and redeems" to resonate in the hearts and minds of the coming generations. And I think it has been far too much displaced, forgotten, or diluted beyond recognition in the recent decades of our denominational preoccupation with success or survival.

Generation X and Generation Y don't read books much, but I wish they would read this one, because my heart is with them. It is among these generations so disconnected from the institutions and traditions of the Christian church, that I anticipate the next great awakening. Their spiritual hungering is palpable, but their cynicism about so much that they see and hear in the religious world is understandable. I believe that it is the very Reformed tradition which we hold that is exactly what their heart seeks.

My wife asked me how much of this book I thought would come true. I responded: "About 85 percent." I stand by that. The collapse of the Enlightenment construct, and the Protestant liberal theology which it generated, along with the ambiguous *postmodern* assumptions that are currently in ascendancy mean that we have more than a little chaos. The end of Christendom and the fact that we are now very much in a neo-pagan mission context brings to an end our urbane "Presbyterian way of life."

My thanks to all of those who have encouraged me to bring this to publication: my pastor Scott Weimer, along with Billy Mitchell, Sam Henderson, Louis Evans, and Bill Welch. Then my gratitude to Sam and Eileen Moffett who put me in touch with Providence House, and the wonderful staff at Providence House for their invaluable assistance and encouragement. May it all be used to encourage, provoke, and equip the saints for the mission into the twenty-first century. And to God be the glory.

"This Old House"

WHAT PROVOKED MY PROJECTING THE FUTURE OF THE Presbyterian Church (U.S.A.) [PC(USA)] into the culture of the twenty-first century was a rude awakening which began several years ago and has been gestating in my psyche with increasing urgency. Eight or nine years ago we had occasion to do what we Presbyterians are good at: namely, realigning and reorganizing presbytery. I was asked to chair the Committee on Mission Design for the new presbytery. This gave us a unique moment to find out where we had consensus as the Presbyterian folk in that region. The committee was a superb bunch—bright, good-humored, and up to the task. We spent several long sessions processing what it meant to be part of the Presbyterian family, and what should be our common understanding of our life and mission.

Guess what? We came up with the fact that our mission is well-defined in the first three chapters of the PC(USA) *Book of Order,* and most specifically that what formed us in our mission was found in chapter 2: "The Church and Its Confessions," i.e., we were formed for mission by our biblical and theological understanding. Our mission was the same as all of the Christian church. After all, there was an abundance of the Episcopal, Methodist, Baptist, Roman Catholic, Assemblies of God, and other church congregations in our region, who also believed in Jesus and the gospel. So, we reported to presbytery that our understanding of mission was that we were to be the presence of a *Reformed understanding of the Christian faith* through our several-score congregations. Sound simple enough?

We therefore asked for a special order at a presbytery meeting to work on this with our elders and pastors. We had a fine group process worked out, with prepared leaders, and all the accoutrements. Again, guess what? Almost *nobody* had a clue what we were talking about! The groups reported that this was all new to them, and a fascinating discovery. Not a clue about Reformed understanding, though every member of that governing body had taken a solemn ordination vow to:

> . . . sincerely receive and adopt the essential tenets of the Reformed faith as expressed in the confessions of our Church as authentic and reliable expositions of what Scripture leads us to believe and do, and [to] be instructed and led by those confessions as [we] lead the people of God.
>
> (Book of Order G–14.0207c)

My inspired thought at that moment? "We've got a big problem!"

So the seed of this book was sown. The disturbing awakening of that day has been exacerbated in the intervening years in conversation after conversation, and in clergy and seminary conferences all across the denomination. For all of our vaunted "connectionalism," it is only our *theological* consensus and our *missional* consensus which are the glue that gives us coherence. It is these that give us integrity in our calling to be about the *Missio Dei*, the mission of God. If there is no consensus on these, then there is nothing that "connects" us. Some would insist that our polity connects us. Not so! Polity only has to do with the form of witness, not the essence. A "denomination" is actually the aggregate of congregations consenting to be accountable to each other in theology and mission. This is good and helpful. But if this *consensus* is absent, then there may still be the same number of congregations, but there is no reason for the denomination.

When our very existence is shot through and through with a lack of integrity on theology and mission, then that leaves us very vulnerable to progressive "dry rot." As a matter of fact, that destructive process is increasingly obvious. Not only is institutional confidence at such a low ebb as to hardly register,[1] but there is a generation of younger adults that are looking at it all with a big "Who needs it?" kind of disdain. When the publicity surrounding every annual General Assembly is either enigmatic, uncertain, or embarrassing, then the rank and file in the pew have legitimate reason to be unconvinced and to wonder why we bother.

WHOOPS! HOLD ON, NOT SO FAST

But wait a minute! It's not all that simple. There's something buried here in this ecclesiastical confusion that must not be lost. There is something, perhaps only slightly visible at the moment, which needs to be more than just rediscovered, it needs to be refounded. That "something" is the Reformed tradition. This thrilling and dynamic window into the Christian faith, and into God's purpose in the world, is our particular gift within the larger family of God. It is this all-encompassing understanding of God's sovereign purpose in Christ which called forth this denominational witness. It may sound like a dreary bit of theological esoterica, visited only by some kind of weird theological elite; perhaps it sounds like the preserve of a special breed of the diligent, the scholarly, who are desperate for something to deliver them from boredom. But it should not be. And so my project.

My young adult friends (the "twenty-something" bunch) are asking the very questions to which the Reformed tradition gives profound answers. Yet this tradition is so buried in ecclesiastical chaos that it is hardly a living voice. So, most have never been exposed to it. Again, this is tragic. This emerging adult generation is not fenced-in by the Presbyterian Church. Not at all. It has no reverence for an institution with an indistinct sound. It will go looking for some thoughtful Christian community which hears its questions and speaks its language, but most of all, a Christian community which takes its Christian faith seriously and thoughtfully and offers hope. The Presbyterian Church is hardly the "only show in town." Worse than that, *it is a non-factor.*

EVANGELIZING THE REFORMED TRADITION

It is because of my great desire for this emerging generation that I want to dig through the rubble, retrieve this enormously wonderful and powerful under-standing of God's design in Christ, and let it speak to a generation screaming in a cultural darkness with little hope. It is a generation that has become immune to inane Christian hucksterism. The other "gospels" of the world which it has tried are proving themselves bankrupt and dead-ended. Meanwhile, the Christian church, for the most part, is lost in another world and speaks another language. Tragically (and what I will call by its classical designation) the Reformed tradition which speaks of transcendence, hope, structure, and true intimacy with God and others, lies hidden even, to the very church which it called into being.

What follows in these pages is an *evangelizing* statement. Let me explain that. The warning messages are all over the screen, namely that we are watching the demise of denominational structures as we have known them. This is especially true of the so-called "mainline" denominations. And this is no great loss. All denominational structures and their institutions can outlive their usefulness. The church of Jesus Christ doesn't come to an end as denominations come and go. It only finds its realization in different forms. The fact is that most folk *within* the PC(USA) cannot give a convincing reason as to why we, as Presbyterians, exist in the first place. Those persons for whom the Presbyterian Church is their whole identity, will kick and scream at such an observation. Nonetheless, history and biblical studies prove the point.

Evangelize is a word that has to do with a thrilling and joyous announcement that is both urgent and convincing. When anything is "evangelized" it is alive, energized, dynamic, compelling, and fraught with anticipation. It is just because of this rich meaning that the New Testament employs the word *gospel* (an English translation of the Greek word *evangel* [ευαγγλιον]), to describe the message of Jesus. The message of Jesus and the kingdom of God are called "the gospel of Jesus Christ" or "the gospel of the kingdom." This was a message of urgency and joy and compelling importance. This being so, to use the verbal form, *evangelize*, is to speak of the dynamic of energizing and persuading some-thing, or someone, of the joy, urgency, and compelling content and importance of a such a thing. My purpose, then, is to *evangelize* the Reformed tradition and to give it some "zing!" I want it to be heard and to be an *evangelizing* force among my friends in the emerging adult generation (and anyone else along the way!). If this can be done, then the PC(USA) has a future.

In these pages, I want to evangelize the Reformed tradition,[2] which is the reason for the very existence of the Presbyterian structure, or denomination. I do not want to evangelize the denomination *qua* "denomination." Denominations, as we have known them, are now anachronistic. But the Reformed tradition is the treasure around which the denomination came into existence, and it is a gift to the whole of the church ("one holy catholic and apostolic"). It is only that this treasure has been so forgotten that it is practically the province of only a select few historians, theologians, and even fewer pastors and leaders (which is the real tragedy). I am not even convinced that this desig-nation, i.e. "Reformed tradition," is a good one, but I don't know what other handle to put on it, so I will use it. But at the same time, I want to assert my conviction that an evangelized, or energized, and alive Reformed tradition will transform existing structures or create new ones to contain it. Even more, it will be a much needed and life-producing blessing to the larger family of God as the twenty-first century unfolds.

A CULTURAL DIASTROPHISM AND JOHN CALVIN

My thesis here is that we are living through what pollster Daniel Yankelovich has called a "cultural diastrophism." A *diastrophism* is that effect produced by the movement and grinding of the giant subterranean tectonic plates, which causes earthquakes and which obliterates all familiar landmarks.[3] My observation is that such cultural change is vigorously resisted and denied by many who are wedded to the present Presbyterian structures. But nothing is exempt from this diastrophism. Nothing. Ways of thinking, intellectual constructs, institutions, political and social structures, traditions, cultural mores—all are in for some inevitable and often drastic change. The church and its institutions are no exception.

It it this inevitability which motivates and evangelizes me to write this. Our Reformed tradition, if you look at its impact in the days of its vigor, was not only a culturally transforming force, but a *culture-creating* force also. It was fascinating for me to stand in the nave of St. Pierre's Church in Geneva, Switzerland, where John Calvin opened up the Word of God in preaching. He is the historic figure who stands large at the beginning of our tradition. He also, like we, in his day stood at the threshold of a time of enormous cultural change (called the Protestant Reformation). He became pastor of that strategic church while in his mid-twenties. By then he had already written a major work on the dimensions of our Christian faith. His vision encompassed the whole of life and of God's creation. To look at that little pulpit in a relatively small nave and to realize that John Calvin, from that forum, created an evangelizing force that impacted not only the church, but the world of politics, eonomics, education, art, and the way of thinking and living, is absolutely thrilling.[4] The culture was never the same after that.

In our own present cultural chaos, emerging as we are out of this diastrophism, it is just such a wholistic understanding of the sovereign good purpose of God in Christ that the "twenty-something" generation desperately needs and is crying out for. It is so radically different from the culture without meaning in which they live, that it bids fair to catch their attention. But tragically, it is just this massive heritage of ours that has been consigned to virtual obscurity,[5] so that as a church we are no longer all that convincing to ourselves or to the culture of darkness in which we are ostensibly the "light."

Please indulge me a bit of latitude here. There is no *generic* Presbyterian Church. I am indulging here in broad-stroked caricature. There are, for all of the forgetfulness and foibles and unfaithfulness within this Presbyterian family, still pockets of Reformed awareness and creativity and life. There are those who quietly and faithfully remember and live out this wonderful tradition. But, "get real!" . . . it gets more and more difficult to find. The Reformed tradition sees life and the world through a special focus. This focus is on the wonderful and majestic Creator God, sovereignly and graciously working out his redeeming purpose in Jesus Christ. The arena of this New Creation is right in the midst of our very real world in which we live, with all of its tragic and dark realities.

This is "the foolishness of our preaching" (1 Cor. 1:21). And because this is so, this Reformed tradition has also been tough-minded and theologically oriented. It takes people seriously, and it takes the world seriously. It has, in its days of vigor, stood in bold missionary confrontation with all of the structures of society. The "church gathered" became the communal context of a kind of disciplemaking and nurture that equipped all of the people of God to function as salt and light in the very real social and political context of darkness that was their daily missionary incarnation. And so they were.

When our Reformed tradition and genius is forgotten, we become little more than custodians of a dubious church institution. When that erosion takes place, we are hardly convincing to ourselves and much less convinced that we have anything to say to those outside. So, it is more than sad. It is tragic. And so it is.

"THIS OLD HOUSE"

Perhaps I can use the public television program "This Old House" as a metaphor for what I think needs to happen. The program's hosts, Steve and Norm, take us week by week to a series of venerable old houses, which in their day were marvelous examples of beauty, architecture, and liveability. They've got history written all over them. The problem is that the years have taken their toll. One ill-conceived or inappropriate addition or remodeling after another has hidden the houses' original beauty and their integrity. Dry rot may have eaten away important joists. We meet the old houses in a state of decay or structural confusion. The question is always whether there is enough inherent value in the basic structure to warrant the considerable expense and labor required to refurbish them. Is there something in this unlikely structure worth saving? Do the immediate shabbiness, absence of insulation, archaic heating and cooling systems, violation of codes in plumbing and electricity, and the lead-based paint and its consequences make the houses viable as a projects for renewal? Or should they be demolished and another started from scratch?

Of course, the houses they choose for the program are always worthy. At great cost and with gifted craftsmenship and patience, they strip away all that is extraneous to the integrity of the structure. Then they go to work to reproduce what they have envisioned. The final product is always a thing of beauty, re-done with excellence for the present and the foreseeable future. But, again, such *refounding into integrity has a high cost.* It has consequences. Everything that is not necessary to its integrity is torn out and disposed of. This means that basic decisions are made to undergo the radical steps necessary to restore the basic integrity of the house. All of the unwanted accretions of the years are consigned to the dumpster.

The "This Old House" metaphor expresses my feeling about the large number of Presbyterian congregations within this denominational family, which do still have basic integrity of ministry, where there is still both a lively pulse and a healthy persuasion of the Reformed tradition. Our Reformed tradition came into being out of a magnificent awakening to the sovereign grace of God irresistibly working out his good and saving purpose in Jesus Christ. It came with a transformational dimension to it that saw all of creation as the area of our missionary calling and our stewardship. It was a reforming force. It has been a light in the cultural darkness time and again and in many contexts.

EVERYBODY WON'T BUY IN

I am not so naive as to think that every congregation is going to gird up its intention and pay the price to become a Reformed community. Not at all. Of our present eleven thousand congregations, many couldn't care less. Many have made a decision only to survive as long as possible as an institution. They have no mission beyond survival. They will die "decently and in order." Others have already set aside their ordination vows and the guidance of the confessions,[6] and are adrift on a sea of theological "deconstruction." Still others profess to be evangelical, but have willingly chosen to mute the difficult demands of the gospel of the Kingdom in order to make their preaching and programs "sell" more easily to the fickle religious masses. Such congregations and teachers don't necessarily say anything heretical, and they do want the church to grow. It is just that they leave out significant and demanding portions of New Testament teachings in the process.

The Reformed tradition has always contained a stubborn sense of the integrity of the biblical message and sought to implement it in all of its thoroughness. It has exalted Christian obedience as the only viable expression of Christian experience. It knows that to love Christ is to keep his commandments, and that "self-fulfillment" therefore is not the goal of Christian discipleship. The work of the Holy Spirit is to create the church as the community of the New Creation. This implies also the Spirit's work of conforming men and women to the likeness of Christ. Such a course is not easy or popular. This "small gate and narrow road" causes many to turn aside and seek an easier way.

Acknowledging that this is true, I am also looking at the cultural signs and recognizing that the name "Presbyterian" means almost nothing to most folk. It certainly does not carry the reputation any longer of being a people of conviction and boldness and holy obedience. What lingers is a sad relic of a former glory. But hidden within this relic is a treasure, and many congregations still cherish it and take it seriously. It is to these that I write. And such *refounding* almost never begins with a decision from the top, but with one or two, with a group, or a class, or a session . . . who begin to pray and study and seek God's face.[7] Then the determination is to obey God and become involved. Little by little, such faithful folk begin to demonstrate life and truth, to gently and patiently and lovingly strip away the decay, and return to the integrity of structure. Blessed *refounders*.

BEYOND RENEWAL TO REFOUNDING

From this point, I want to deliberately employ the term *"refound"* to express the goal of this *Blueprint 21* project. It is a term which I have borrowed from Gerald Arbuckle, whose work I have greatly appreciated. He is a missionary and a cultural anthropologist who writes from within the Roman Catholic tradition.[8] Arbuckle insists that the word "renew" is quite too weak to express what needs to happen when any Christian movement lets its founding *raison d'être* (its core of understanding and values and mission) become diluted, displaced, or forgotten. When that happens, he observes, "order" devolves into "chaos." So the term *refound* denotes an intentional return to the foundation upon which the church (community or denomination) is founded so that it can be a viable witness for present and future. That is exactly what I propose for our *Reformed house*. I look upon the Presbyterian form of government only secondarily (and non-essentially), since Reformed convictions are held by many in other traditions (such as Baptist and Methodist, among others).[9]

The *Reformed* understanding of the Christian faith is our "wine" and the Presbyterian form of government is only the "wineskin" which we have chosen to employ as its vehicle. Ironically, a wineskin can exist without the wine but the reverse is not true. Without a wineskin the wine is lost. So we need wineskins, but primarily to be adequate vessels of the content. They are not an end in themselves. So the word is *refound*. I shall employ it henceforth as we look at our biblical and theological "wine" and at what will be needed to give it form in its mission in the world, its "wineskin."

THE POST-DENOMINATIONAL ERA

We are at the *twilight of denominations*. The PC(USA) has a very limited future in its present state, as do all denominations.[10] This Message Box looms large on the screen of all appraisals of the days ahead. The days of the "mainline" denominations are rather like recent news reports about the 120-year-old lady in France. When a reporter asked what her plans for the future were, she replied: "Limited." The problem is that most of the mainline denominations have been around for so long that they have forgotten exactly why they exist in the first place. Congregations may take pride in their particular institutions but are little more than denominational franchises with no particular self-understanding of why they wear the particular labels they do within the larger "holy catholic church." Add to that another Message Box on the screen, namely that denominations are a *non-factor* in the minds of the emerging adult generation.

This forgetfulness of our Reformed *founding myth* is exacerbating our own denominational *chaos*. Presbyterians have pretty much forgotten the genius of the Reformed faith, our heritage from John Calvin, and his biblical-theological progeny. So also have the children of John Wesley, Martin Luther, and other such formative voices from the past. This is true also of Roman Catholic and Eastern Orthodox traditions. Such forgetfulness is what makes *post-denominationalism* our present reality. How we all "fit" and "belong" and minister to one another symbiotically within the larger Body of Christ is hardly discussed or understood by ordinary folk in the pew. This may not be all bad. Lesslie Newbigin, who is a giant in his own right, quotes with approbation another notable, H. Richard Niebuhr, in asserting that, "Denominationalism represents the moral failure of Christianity."[11]

Our Reformed missiological and theological definition must be refounded. Realignments will be necessary. All kinds of things are possible. Perhaps in the days ahead the doors between traditions will swing both ways, so that at a given time and in given circumstances, congregations may well choose to identify with some other tradition. If congregations from other denominations are Reformed in ministry and should consent to share mission with us, why not?[12] Or if some of "our" congregations no longer have any affinity for the Reformed faith and wished to identify with a Wesleyan body, is this sin? Not at all. There should be an orderly way for this to happen.[13]

Factor in the realization that most folk who join the Presbyterian Church today do not do so because of its theology or its church government, but only because they find something within that particular congregation that attracts them. That something may be the people, personality of the pastor, location, programs, priorities, message and preaching, or perhaps the style of worship (or its church basketball team!). But it is seldom because of anything to do with "Reformed" understanding of the Christian faith, which is our denominational *raison d'être*. Folks easily move from one Christian tradition, or denomination, to another and even between Catholicism and Protestantism without a qualm.

Denominational names are not only confusing but often a stumbling block for the generation of young adults today. All of this will become much more obvious as we move into the twenty-first century.

The generation emerging into adulthood today (of which I will speak significantly in the next chapter) has hardly a shred of denominational or institutional interest, much less loyalty. If one of them were to ask what in the world a *Presbyterian* was, and we were to properly answer that we are a community of Christians governed by *presbyters*, or elders, he or she would more than likely respond in some disbelief and cynicism, "Yeah, right. Well, *whoop-dee-doo!*" And walk off, leaving us standing there in dismay. The church is now looking at a generation of disillusioned and spiritually hungry young adults who have been raised in an almost completely secular culture. It is our first *neo-pagan* and *post-modern* generation. It is a generation of cynicism, of distrust of institutions (denominations, again, are a *non-factor*), of promises given and not kept. It is a disconnected generation without absolutes—moral or otherwise—and without a sense of future and hope. It is also a generation who, for the most part, have never experienced intimacy in family. Their *self-fulfillment* "Boomer" parents didn't let children interfere with their own professional or personal ambitions and so created a generation of emotional orphans, abandoned to fend for themselves in the dominant social order of secularism.

At the same time, as I have suggested, it is a generation looking for the very realities which our Christian faith professes to believe and incarnate. If we had replied to the same "What is a *Presbyterian?*" question above with a bit more of a sensitive answer, we might have sustained the young person's attention. We might have proposed,

> Well, now that you ask, we're something like a family of Christian folk, which began in a period not unlike this one. After a long period of sort of hopeless cultural darkness, our spiritual ancestors rediscovered the God who had visited humankind in Jesus Christ. The more they looked, the more they saw that this God was really God, that he took both them and the world very seriously. What they discovered was that God loved them and invited them into his family and his sovereign purpose for the world. They rediscovered in God that there is hope and joy and meaning in this very real world in their lives. You cannot imagine how freeing and motivating this was. The more they looked into the records of God's working, and at Jesus, God's son, the more they found it all true, and life took on a whole new dimension. They were empowered to begin to live different kinds of lives and to make a difference in society. They became a community. The awkward name *Presbyterian* simply explains that our family is given structure and caring by wonderful men and women who are models and mentors, called "elders," (from the Greek word *presbyter*). But what gives us our

life together and our joy is Jesus, God's gift of life to us. There! That's more than you wanted, but you asked, so I've answered.

. . . Something like that. If we came forth with that kind of answer, we just *might* punch a few buttons, get a hearing, and the conversation just might go on.

BUT DENOMINATIONS WON'T VANISH

This is beginning to sound like a broken record, but denominations have pretty much "lost it" when it comes to knowing why they exist. This is obviously true of us who are Presbyterians. But even as I suggest that denominations *qua* denominations have a limited future, I hardly believe that they will simply vanish; however, it is hardly conceivable that they will look at all the same twenty years from now. The focus will come back to the local congregations. Vital congregations in all of these traditions will find (and are already finding) each other. They will "network" to accomplish mutual goals. But they will do this in a much different way than current denominational structures and hierarchies function.

No matter what transpires in the Presbyterian denomination, its governing bodies, and its administrative structures in the near future, there will still be something like eleven thousand congregations who are identified with the PC(USA). Of these I would estimate (though no one really knows) that maybe two-thirds are probably viable as Christian communities, i.e., still have a good pulse.[14] Sadly, some will be only relics existing on past momentum but without any vital life signs.

This "old Reformed house" contains a theological structure and a witness desperately needed in this emerging postmodern culture. Sadly, though, it is too often hidden beneath layers of ecclesiastical accretions, or structural gewgaws, so that it is all-but-forgotten. Within the larger Christian family, it is the tradition that has most wonderfully exhibited an intellectual toughness and a transformational devotion to Christ which has influenced all that it touched. It has done this through disciplined lives and disciplined minds in the people of faith. It has done this in the economy, the body politic, humane interests, education, and social environment, as well as the church. It is, after all, this *wholistic understanding of the gospel of God* which is our true heritage and our reason for being a denomination. But years of good intentions and convenient-but-incompatible additions and innovations have combined with decay and forgetfulness and biblical illiteracy to bring us to this present dilemma. The question becomes: Is there something in this chaos worth salvaging in a post-denominational culture?

Yes, and again, a most emphatic yes!

A TWENTY-FIRST CENTURY NEIGHBORHOOD

My conviction is also that *if* this "old Reformed house" is refounded in its integrity, it will find itself in *a twenty-first century neighborhood of other splendid houses* also in process of being refounded to their original integrity. They may or may not have their family name emblazoned on the door, but the doors will be open. They will be Wesleyan, Anglican, Roman Catholic, Mennonite, Lutheran, Orthodox, Pentecostal, and Independent houses (and some that we haven't even heard of yet). They will be wonderfully cosmopolitan in their make-up. Their children will play together in each other's backyards. All of these will share their rich family heritage with the others, but each will know and take pride in what its family heritage is. And their common heritage of biblical narrative will be celebrated. Family members will know that they are heirs of all of these traditions within the larger "one holy catholic and apostolic church," as well as their own. They will break the bread and drink from the cup together. Together they will seek to be the Lord's missionary incarnation in the midst of a very dark and complex cultural and contextual neighborhood. In the twenty-first century, please take note, our neighborhoods will probably no longer be congenial to the Christian message. The missionary context will be very real and challenging.

One thing is for sure. The church of the next century will not look like the church of the past century. "This is not your father's Oldsmobile," goes the commercial. Theologian (and maverick) Stanley Hauerwas puts it more bluntly, "God is killing the mainline denominations, and damn well should!" Who knows? He could be right. However one observes our present Presbyterian state, it reminds one of the late humorist Lewis Grizzard's lament, "Elvis is dead, and I ain't feelin' so well myself!" It is a fact of church history that congregations and churches can and do die. Christian communities are viable only so long as they are faithful to the one who builds the church, Jesus Christ. Else, as the ascended Lord reminded the churches of Asia Minor, "I will remove your lamp from the lampstand" (Rev. 2–3). So it behooves us to come humbly and honestly back to scripture, to church history, and to the realities of the missionary context of our own culture. We are entering the twenty-first century and desperately need to be architects of the Presbyterian church in a post-denominational age. We need to be faithful in encouraging each other as we hold on to what is good. At the same time, we need to deliberately begin dismantling that which hinders obedience and fruitfulness and violates the integrity of "this old Reformed house" in our missionary encounter with the world, which is our neighborhood.

The late John Mackay of Princeton commented that he would not be surprised if the future of the church did not belong either to "a reformed Catholicism, or a matured Pentecostalism—or a combination of the two!" He could have been prophetic. What we need is, at once, a deep rootedness within the valid traditions and history of the "holy, catholic church." At the same time, we need the capacity of being open to the creativity and empowering of the Creator Spirit in an unfamiliar culture now intruding upon us. It is in this task that we Reformed folk should understand our principle: *Ecclesia reformata, semper reformanda,* . . . the church reformed, always reforming (*Book of Order,* G–2.0200).

So what have we got to work with? Look at some pieces with me.

WHAT HAVE WE GOT?

On paper we have something like 2.5 million Presbyterian folk. But what does that mean? It means that we have a huge diversity of people in both faith and lack of faith. When one of my friends called the church a "zoo," he intended to be humorous, but he was far more descriptive than he imagined. Anyone of us who has been around the church for very long, and who has paid his or her dues in leadership in session and presbytery, can identify some of the following specimens in our Presbyterian zoo. For nearly every description of individuals which follows, there is probably a congregation type that is similar. There are those:

- people who live in different communities of understanding and subcultures of ideology, prejudice, social, economic, and ethnic orders;
- people who are wedded to the Presbyterian Church "that was" (say, in 1975) and have a difficult time countenancing anything (like this document) which questions it;
- people for whom the church is part of their social fabric and their comfortable context, but who hardly take seriously faith and discipleship. These are the passive "church goers," who seem not to have a thought about the church's mission or its understanding of the Christian faith, and are perennially biblical illiterates;
- people who have inherited a Presbyterian pedigree and participated in its institutions, but who have never been captured by Jesus Christ and are essentially "unconverted believers";
- people and congregations who are self-consciously evangelical but not Reformed, and those, conversely, who are self-consciously Reformed but do not identify themselves as evangelical;
- people who are committed to Presbyterian polity, and so take the confessions as part of the package, but without much sense of their content or the vitality of an obedient faith;

- naive, "go-with-the-flow"/"every-wind-of-doctrine," folk who just "like the church," and are among its most regular attendees, but remain strangers to the "doing of the Word," i.e., passive attendees who come to be inspired;
- people who have long since rejected or reinterpreted the normativeness of scripture, so that it has no authority in life and faith (assuming they know its content). These have also, when ordained by this stance, set aside their ordination vows regarding scripture, and so stepped outside of the confessional family;
- people who are heirs of the "Find God at work in the world and join him there" legacy, whose theological stance seems to change with every new socio-political *zeitgeist* that comes along;
- people who are socio-political conservatives who identify stability with their version of Christianity, and those other conservatives who see every cultural aberration as a threat and a Satanic assault (but who at least take the biblical faith seriously, if not maturely!);
- pathological individuals who seek leadership to be in positions of power and control and employ the means to achieve it;
- people who are the "wheat and the tares" of Jesus' parable, growing together in the same field, the same church; it is not at all easy to discern which is which, but it is not ours to be judges; instead we know it is true and accept the reality of an imperfect church;
- people who are "custodians of the institution" who seem only concerned with the survival and prosperity of the institutional wineskin but are (to all appearances) unaware of its *raison d'être* and are too frequently strangers to scripture (and too frequently inhabit the committees and councils of the governing bodies, alas!);
- cerebral type persons who are always raising questions, analyzing proposals, and reading new studies, but are not of much practical help in making it all happen;
- expediters who, with devotion and skill, are the working heart of any vital congregation, who, in fact, are the ministers of "energy, intelligence, imagination, and love," and so give the church that life and love that manifests the Spirit of God in its midst;
- persons who are that necessary minority of visionaries and futurists, looking at the present and the future and trying to figure how to get there from here with that same "energy, intelligence, imagination, and love."

But . . .

- . . . then, I would suspect that the majority, the more silent majority, are those who are simply folk of good will and true faith in God's love and purpose in

Christ, and who accept the fact that the church is somehow the community of faith, hope, and love. These are the salt-of-the-earth saints who quietly worship and serve and love out of sight, but give one great encouragement in this pilgrimage.

- Mix into all of this the fact that some in the church are quite too suspicious of everything and everyone, lest somehow I, and we, should become tainted with something heterodox, and so are ever looking for culprits to blame. These keep everyone else on edge. Then there are their counterparts who are, conversely, too trusting, believing the very best of everyone in the church without any healthy and realistic discernment of the subtleties that have always taken and continue to take the church off into alien paths. Somewhere in the middle should be a healthy mix of discernment and love, which doesn't fall off too far in either direction.

- Then, take note—there are all of those who have found the message of Jesus and new life in the context of the Presbyterian family. They may have wandered in off the street, or been befriended by some Presbyterian person, but their immediate birthright is within a Presbyterian congregation, and they feel a sense of indebtedness and loyalty to that church.

Our Presbyterian zoo is a fascinating mix of these different personalities. Some are charming and way off base. Some are obstreperous but have hearts and minds that are wedded to scripture and that belong to Christ. So it is and has always been. So where are we?

PRESENT CHAOS

If Yankelovich's term "diastrophism" doesn't convey the picture of our present scene to you, then perhaps the example of the recent Hurricane Andrew will make it clearer. That destructive hurricane blew through south Miami and not only destroyed the homes, but it took away all of the street signs and stop lights so that there was no way to identify one's own neighborhood. Such drastic events and cultural shifts are so very difficult to conceive when everything in our daily lives seems so normal, so much the same, and so familiarly routine. Oh, occasionally we get some uneasy feeling that things aren't quite as they should be, and certainly are not as they used to be. Still, the hurricane warnings have been coming and the cultural winds have blown, and though all may visibly look the same, they are not. And the twenty-first century will surely be an increasing manifestation of that fact.

This is just to say that the Presbyterian Church, in its present state, is feeling that cultural diastrophism. The older generation (my generation) clings to memories of the Presbyterian Church that *was* twenty to thirty years ago. I recently attended a conference of Presbyterian church leaders. Present were some very gifted pastors and lay persons from significant congregations. Some of them were sitting informally after a meal, chatting about this very subject. When the question came up, "How long do you give this denomination?" the answer came—"Five or six years." Nobody in that group would have been considered a radical. All were there as loyal and gifted participants in this denomination's leadership. None would want to go on record as having given this answer, but, in the anonymity of an informal session, their "gut feelings" responded honestly.

An increasing number of significant congregational leaders and conscientious Christian laypersons, question the whole denominational structure, including the meetings of the General Assembly, as having no relevance to anything they are involved in as Christians. This Message Box appears regularly on the screen of normal conversations within the family.

Another episode is illustrative. At a church-related college, a new chaplain had sensed the true spiritual hungerings of a student body of typical middle-class church kids. They had resisted the college's twice weekly (and stiflingly formal) chapel services as "unreal." The new chaplain, who was most gifted in communicating with such youth, instituted chapel services to speak to them musically as well as verbally. When their kind of music conveyed the message, and when one who was sensitive to their cultural questions and realities was able to communicate the Christian message with humor and conviction, the chapel services became a "standing room only" phenomena! A spiritual awakening took place on what had been a jaded and "turned-off" scene.

When some older elders from supporting congregations approached the chaplain, they were not convinced. "These large crowds are fine, but tell us— what are you doing to prepare these young people for our churches?" When reporting this encounter to me, the chaplain grinned and said, "I didn't have the heart to tell them that these young people weren't going to go to their churches!" The reason? This new generation is not going to find its intense spiritual hungerings met in churches that exist simply to exist, without sensitivity to the spiritual pilgrimage of folk who are different.

POSTMODERN ERA

Those who study such abstract disciplines as cultural trends and philosophical shifts call this new setting without landmarks *postmodernism*. Without trying to confuse my readers with the more esoteric and sophisticated details, *postmodernism* simply does not accept a lot of things which the *modern* era took for granted, i.e., "the domination of nature, the primacy of method, and the sovereignty of the individual."[15] Add to this several assumptions about the place of reason in determining reality, the scientific method as determinative of truth, the inevitability of progress, and the role and reliability of many social, religious, and governmental institutions. These assumptions are not accepted by the postmodern mind. I think it was Gertrude Stein (or maybe comedian Woody Allen) who lamented that "There is no *there* there!" That is a fairly accurate description of *postmodernism*. There is no continuity and no center. History is "de-constructed." Everything is rather up-for-grabs.

Attempting to put dates on such things is difficult. One observer suggested that the *modern* era began with Columbus' discovery of a new world and came crashing down with the fall of the Berlin Wall. Within those general parameters, the intellectual principles of the Enlightenment (of philosophers Descartes, Locke, Hume, Kant, etc.) pretty much determined the culture. The industrial revolution, technology, both capitalism and communism as economic systems, theological developments, and urbanization—with all of the implications of these—were the fruits of, or significantly influenced by, the Enlightenment. So also, in theology, was Protestant Liberalism, which dominated the church for too much of the twentieth century.

No more. Face a culture and a younger generation which are not convinced of, nor formed by, those *modern* assumptions and you are looking at life through a whole different set of eyes.

You are looking at a generation of young women and men who are less than convinced that the *modern* era of their parents was all that good. They see environmental pollution, greed and deception in government, the depersonalization of society—to mention a few—as the results of that very era. Therefore, the institutions of that era, such as the church and the government, are somewhat suspect and looked upon cynically.

FORGETFULNESS

Within the Presbyterian Church, a considerable part of the *chaos* is simply *forgetfulness*. This is nothing new among God's people. It was forgetfulness that undid ancient Israel. It has happened again and again in church history. But it is now so very obvious within the Presbyterian family. Ordinary Presbyterian folk hardly have a memory of why it is that we exist as a particular people within the mission of God. Oh, the initial statements in our constitutional *Book of Order* are magnificent, but they are also hardly taken into account. Look at the denominational journals, and what do you find? Not excitement about the gospel of God, our thrilling mission in the world, the riches and action-implications of Reformed thought, or even about the profound riches of scripture. Nor do you have reports of the thousands of Presbyterian laity who are living out a thrilling witness in America's everyday life.

Rather, what you ordinarily find in church publications is a succession of dismal reports about housekeeping details, committees appointed, budget crises, or about petty controversies over polity. The focus is on the "old wineskin" rather than on the intoxicating "new wine of the gospel." In a real sense, our chaos began when the "wineskin" (which was created only to be a vessel of the true wine of the gospel of the dominion of God), took on a life of its own and preempted the place of focus. So, in reality, we have two Presbyterian churches. One is the church formed by scripture and theology and focused on the missional mandate of Jesus Christ. The other is that one which is consumed by polity, with its omnivorous capacity to consume personnel, money, and time apart from the mission of God.

Add to that forgetfulness and a resultant indifference to the essence and exclusivity of Christian faith and witness, namely, *pluralism*. There is a doorway into God's new creation in Christ—into his great salvation—and that doorway is by *repentance* toward God and *faith* in Jesus Christ. So, also, entrance into leadership in the Presbyterian family is by ordination vows which require that biblical and Reformed beliefs are determinative of our life together. Both of these doorways are exclusive. God's invitation to "whosoever will" is to step over this threshold, and until those outside do so, they are still outside. But when *valid diversity* within the family becomes *pluralism* in which there are no standards of faith or conduct, no truth and error, then *chaos* results. The end result of pluralism is most strikingly caricatured in the report of a group of Anglican priests who accused the church of religious discrimination.

> The Bishop of Chichester, England, dismissed an Anglican priest, who does not believe that God exists. The priest, Anthony Freeman, has written: "There is nothing out there—or if there is, we can have no knowledge of it." In a letter protesting the dismissal, sixty-five other priests complained that this "reverses a long Church of England tradition that tolerates and values a wide range of views."[16]

Does one laugh or weep? These same priests took ordination vows of Christian faith as interpreted by the church's strong theological heritage in the Thirty-nine Articles of the Church of England. Is their protest ridiculous? Of course it is. There are outside limits to the Christian faith, and "diversity" has parameters. We Presbyterian folk need to remember and reclaim that which we are. In a very healthy and biblical sense, we are an exclusive community. At our entrance by the waters of baptism or confirmation, we "renounce" the dominion of darkness and unbelief and embrace life under the Lordship of Jesus Christ. We are a community of faith, and that faith has deep roots in the narrative and faith of scriptures.

But we forget!

We have even had to convene a special "Conference on Christology" recently to remind ourselves of the church's faith in Jesus as both truly man and truly God, as set forth in the Creed of Nicea. So essential. So determinative. And yet it has grown dim in the corporate mind of the Presbyterian Church. The conference was a clarion call to "Remember!" It is useless to continue this lament and to enumerate the dimensions of the chaos. It is enough to say that if this "old Reformed house" is to have new life and usefulness in the twenty-first century, then all of these detrimental components must be flagged by our architect so that they can be removed without compromising the integrity of the house.

BUT THERE ARE HEALTHY SIGNS

In the very midst of all of the above, with the discouragements they bring, we do need to remember that the building of the church is ultimately the work of Jesus Christ. We need to be reminded that there is abundant good news and many causes of great encouragement within the family. We dare not overlook all of that healthy life and witness which continues faithful in the midst of it all. While six hundred Presbyterian commissioners meeting at the annual General Assembly may get all of the press coverage of what current controversy the PC(USA) is dealing with this year, that same press fails to cover what the other 2.5 million Presbyterians are doing as the salt of the earth and the light of the world. Nor does the press report what ministries of life and caring are being produced by thousands of congregations across the nation, and, through them, around the world every day.

So before we conclude this chapter, let's look at just some of the evidences of God at work which need to rejoice us and for which we need to give thanks (and take some pride).

• First, look again at the constitutional documents which focus on the glory of God and God's extravagant grace in Christ. Look at how the *Book of Order* opens with a statement about the church as the creation of Jesus Christ and with its missionary purpose in that classic "The Great Ends of the Church."

Look at the following two chapters on what the church believes and the unique set of Reformed tenets. Then look at the chapter on "The Church and It's Mission," and you will have great reason to rejoice and hopefully get excited about God's purpose for the Presbyterian witness in the next century. These are valid foundations for our *refounding* efforts.

- Look at the fruitfulness of our missionary ministry, which continues to surprise us with miracles of grace. Seed sown a century ago bears fruit in places apparently unreachable and impossible. Presbyterian missions are being blessed of God in places unreached until recently. The ministry of Presbyterian Frontier Fellowship within our Worldwide Ministries Division during these recent years in nothing less than thrilling. This is not even to mention what presbyteries and congregations are doing now in mission teams locally and abroad.

- Look at the wave of bright, young, pragmatic, evangelical, and Reformed men and women emerging out of seminaries and into pastoral leadership. You will see a whole new breed who *are* alert to the cultural realities discussed above, and who *are* already refounding congregational "old houses" everywhere and networking with each other in order to encourage each other. These give me hope for the church's witness in the twenty-first century.

- Look at God's "left-handed" surprises. Look at the brilliant Reformed thinkers inhabiting the faculties of major universities, even of Roman Catholic Notre Dame University. Or look at the motherlode of Reformed creativity coming out of Eastern College (which is American Baptist). Who would have thought? This is not to overlook signs of hope in our own colleges and seminaries.

- Look at the triennial Urbana Missionary Conventions (sponsored by Inter-Varsity Christian Fellowship), which are the largest missionary gatherings in the history of the Christian church. For the last couple of decades, records show that of the fifteen thousand-plus students who have gathered for these intense looks at the missionary mandate of the Christian church, the largest denominational representation has been from the PC(USA). This says that something is going on within an emerging generation which is fraught with potential in the whole world.

- Look at the fact that many of the most fruitful parachurch ministries and missionary movements, who are faithfully doing the work of Jesus Christ in the world, are not only led by Presbyterians, but are staffed and supported to a remarkable degree by Presbyterian folk, e.g., World Vision, Inter-Varsity Christian Fellowship, and Young Life to name a few. If all of our PC(USA) communicants who are serving in the mission of the church were considered our missionary force, the PC(USA) is probably one of the largest missionary organizations in the world.

- Or look back to 1985 at the Presbyterian Congress on Renewal, when eight thousand Presbyterians gathered in Dallas, Texas, to celebrate our Reformed faith, and to see models of fruitful ministry in 125 workshops. At the conclusion, the editor of a major publishing house told the leadership team that there had not been an aggregation of evangelical leadership such as that in this century, and what was amazing was that it was all Presbyterian (U.S.A.).[17]

NOW TO THE TASK

What we need to do now is to proceed to define that which is the *sine qua non* of this Presbyterian Church's life and witness. We need to look for that inner integrity of obedience in mission and faithfulness in theology, which will give this Presbyterian family its dynamics for the demands of the twenty-first century and for its unique witness in the *post-denominational* era. What connects Presbyterian congregations is (1) a consensus on our theological understanding and (2) on our mission. Sadly, our chaos at this point results from the obvious fact that we have no overall denominational consensus on these two essentials. Whatever is to be *refounded* will have to *refound* this consensus, and this will undoubtedly not take place without some pain.

Being *pathfinders* out of the chaos always brings resistance from the chaos itself. Folk tend to cling to whatever stability the past gave them and to resist criticism of the present, even when it is obviously moribund. Some fragmentation is to be expected. Change comes hard. But our insistence on our mission and confessions must be with consummate love and sensitivity, and at the same time, with forthrightness. In a real sense, our task is to *evangelize* afresh the Presbyterian presence within the "one holy catholic and apostolic church."

And to do that, we begin with the fact that the Presbyterian Church of integrity is a *missional* community and not a *custodial* community. The mission of God given to us by Jesus Christ is dynamic and must continually renew our minds and determine our life as community. That is the basic principle upon which we begin our architecting of the plan to *refound* "this old house."

WHERE DOES THIS BEGIN?

Like our descent into the present chaos, the church's *refounding* will not be a "program" or an instant-fix solution. It will take time and patience. It begins with a person, then a few persons, then a class or a praying group, who will begin to study the dynamics.[18] Such a group understanding the reality of God's intent for his people and modeling it for the larger church is proven effective back through the church's history. The larger church needs to see the reality of the model of a smaller church, i.e., *ecclesiola in ecclesiam*. Those genuinely concerned cannot wait for something to change from on high, but in humility and gentleness they show their love for Christ and his church as with servant spirits, and they begin to be God's *refounded* church.

My writing of this guide is intended to be a resource for such beginnings. The awakening of the church almost never begins from the top down. It also almost never happens to the whole church at once. The dynamics of *refounding* are somewhat like the New Testament parable of the kingdom of God being like a little leaven growing in a lump of dough. Little by little, with much patience and prayer, it begins to transform. I would hope that you and your group, class, or session might make this a beginning place, and with this book, keep your Bible, *Book of Order*, and *Book of Confessions* by your side as major resources. I will try to footnote some cogent references along the way. Above all, invoke the sweet and life-giving Spirit of God to enable you.

In the next three chapters, I want to attempt to open up three major areas that are *absolutely* (and I mean absolutely) foundational: (1) the focus on God's mission to his lost creation in Christ; (2) the focus on Christ, who is God's good news, with some of the wholistic implications of that; and (3) the focus of our Reformed thought in the sovereign good purpose of God. Only then can we get into some of the implications of that for the *refounded* congregation. May God give us grace in this thrilling and dangerous sojourn.

Veni Creator Spiritus.

Mission: Where the Darkness Is the Greatest

IF THE ONLY REASON WE ARE CONCERNED TO *REFOUND* "THIS old Reformed/Presbyterian house" is to assure the continued institutional existence of these eleven thousand "denominational franchises," then Stan Hauerwas's dire prediction about "God . . . killing the mainline denominations, and damn well should!" is appropriate. The only reason for the existence of these, or any other congregations, is to be the *communities of worship and of costly missional obedience* to our living and risen Lord Jesus Christ, who has called us for this purpose. To be called by Christ is to accept his "As the Father has sent me, even so I am sending you" mission. Otherwise, the Spirit is quenched and we become the "wicked and unfaithful servants" who ignore, if not disobey, the express calling to "show forth the praises of him who called us out of darkness and into his marvelous light" (1 Peter 2:9). Our desire for *refounding* these congregations is to make our Savior's heart glad—to cause God to sing over us for joy.[1] Nothing less.

This is no calling for the complacent, the timid, or those lacking in compassion. There was a remarkable awakening among the youth culture of this nation, known as "The Jesus Revolution," in the early 1970s. One of the thrilling scenes of this awakening was in Berkeley, California, which had also been the focal point of much of the student protest movement of those days. I spent a couple of weeks in the midst of that amazing scene, having my own eyes opened to the power of God. I watched God wonderfully awaken and call forth faith in Jesus Christ in a most unlikely scene of intellectual and moral darkness. In a private moment, I asked one of the leaders, "How do you explain this whole phenomenon?" I share his response with you for our own task here. He said, "I believe that God rejoices to work and show his power where the darkness is the greatest! If you need a text, try 'Where sin increased, grace increased all the more, . . .'" (Rom. 5:20). Though this may be taken slightly out of context, the history of missions corroborates that God has a surprising way of *showing up* where we would least expect and where the effects of the darkness are the most tragic.

PREREQUISITES TO ACTION

It is the acceptance of Christ's calling to be just such communities of gospel and of missionary obedience which will energize the *refounding* of the congregations of the PC(USA), or of any other tradition, in the days ahead. Right away, if we are serious about the task of *refounding* the Presbyterian Church and its congregations for mission in the twenty-first century, there are a couple of things that are absolutely *prerequisite to our initiating any concrete action.*

1. We must be utterly convinced of how desperately, tragically, and heartbreakingly lost is this rebellious creation, and how essential in the purpose of God is the church's role in its redemption. And, . . .
2. any serious intention to *refound* "This Old House" into integrity and fruitfulness must be motivated by nothing less than sheer and profound devotion to Jesus Christ. Any other motivation is simply spurious. By "profound devotion" I mean that before we begin to look at the form of our life together, we must engage in that focused and reflective worship of Jesus Christ and that thoughtful study of scripture, which shall take us deeply into who he is, why he came, how his heart beats, how he sees what we see, how he loves this tragically screwed-up world, what he thinks and wills, and also how he weeps over its lostness. Only then will we begin to see why he calls out a people (an *ecclesia*/a church) and what his purpose and mission for this people is. Only then will we be able to see how this company of men and women are bonded to him in his "seeking and saving the lost." Only then will our calling, forgiveness, newness, and receiving of God's promises bring us to our knees in adoration, but it will energize us to the costly obedience which will make us visibly "the body of Christ" in the world.

OUT OF THE FATHER'S HEART: COMPASSION

Which of these two prerequisites stands first in priority? I am not sure. It is a "chicken or egg" question. However, I want to deliberately create a *mission-focused* context for all that follows, as we move into the next century. So, the second of these I propose to engage in the next chapter. There I want, with you, to "marinate" in the infinite love and extravagant grace of God in Jesus Christ. But the instant you even get close to that theme, you are looking right into the intense compassionate heart of God. Somehow to gaze upon the glory of God in the face of Jesus Christ (2 Cor. 4:6), is to see one whose mission was to "seek and rescue the lost." You see one who looks with boundless love upon his creation, with all of its aberrations and desperate lostness. You see the heart of God who with prodigal love[2] sees a humankind which has missed the whole point of its own being, but which flails about with false quests, bankrupt agendas, and endless "new solutions" to assuage the homelessness of its own heart.

"LOST" IS A GOOD WORD FOR IT

At some point, we have got to come to grips with this reality of *lostness,* of the tragic darkness, despair, and destruction that is pervasive of this human scene. The Creator-Father sees this rebel creation which has no true *being* apart from himself, which has no *meaning* apart from himself, which has no *hope* other than his life-giving breath. He sees the futility of men and women seeking life and reality apart from the only true Source and Light. The Father-Mother compassion of God sees the *age of this cosmos* (Eph. 2:2) consigning itself to its own condemnation (cf. John 3:18–19), yet loves it still and sends the Son to bring salvation.

It is not even useful to engage in esoteric theological debates about "universalism," about our belief or disbelief in "eternal damnation," or any such wanderings on the boundaries of the mystery of God at this point. What we do know is that from first to last the scriptures are unmistakable in their assertion that something is tragically wrong, that this creation has "fallen," and that the consequences call forth both the relentless justice and the infinite mercy of God. From first to last, God makes known a purpose of bringing it all back to himself. With all of the questions which can be asked, God declares a missionary intention in the early pages of the Bible and elects a Middle Eastern sheik, Abraham (c. 2000 B.C.E.), as the instrument by which to initiate it. "In your seed all the nations of the earth shall be blessed."

Through the pages of our biblical narrative, we see God angry at the violations of his glory in his creation, and at the same time we see the God who knows that he himself is the "heart's true home" for all of humankind. He, therefore, is patient and gracious to an undeserving humankind, ever intruding words of invitation to return, as well as words of grace, hope, and future. But the *demonically energized* presence of malignant, eroding, and alienating evil is also unmistakable throughout the warp and woof of human history. Yet, . . . yet, . . . God so loves the world. And so must we. If there is any group to whom frighteningly severe words of judgment come in scripture, it is to those who should know better—those who call Jesus Lord, but do not obey (Matt. 7:21–23). Or those who do not obey the gospel (2 Thess. 1:8b).

It is a struggle for us to escape from our own very darkened human finiteness and to try to look into the heart of the Father. But in Jesus we see clearly enough the intense pangs in the Creator's heart, whose creation it all is and whose we all are. We see humankind so missing the whole point (i.e., falling short of the glory) of its Creator and of his creation and messing it all up so badly, that it becomes tragically lost and blinded and homeless. We see it in all of its destructive agendas and its indifference to the injustices. We see the divisions and hatred that produce such things as genocide and "ethnic cleansing."

The word *sin* has become so abused that it hardly conveys the tragedy. Such a venerable theological definition as "total depravity," if it is even used anymore, is bandied about so carelessly and heartlessly that it becomes an obscene expression in and of itself. Yet even the most secularized pagan knows that something is desperately wrong. She knows that there is some malignancy in the culture that breeds alienation. He knows that there is some virus in the social fabric which evidences itself in the daily news. We look with despair at all of the reports of individual and corporate pessimism and calamity. The New Testament names this dominant social order "the aeon of this cosmos" (Eph. 2:2), i.e., an age and a creation divorced from its creator, inhabited by some kind of a cultural malignancy. The narrative also talks about the kind of moral and spiritual bondage in which men and women live. It talks about lives with passions run amok. It describes the bleak hopelessness that is the life style of this world order. Even the apparently smug, happy-go-lucky, godless pagan experiences cloak an aching emptiness. A generation ago, a poet lamented, "It has been lonely in the world since God died!" And so it would be if God had died!

A CALLING TO MISSIONAL OBEDIENCE TO GOD

The *Incarnate Word*, Jesus, was given for the world. Moreover, he was sent on a specific mission by the Father. He was sent into the darkness. His incarnation was in the midst of the realities of human lostness. But please note the missional focus in Jesus. He was always intensely self-conscious that the works that he was about were not self-conceived but were the works of his Father in heaven. This is nowhere more obvious than in his prayer to the Father near the end of his earthly life (John 17), "I have brought you glory on earth by completing the work you gave me to do." The work, of course, was to ". . . come, bringing salvation." He was the Missio Dei, God's mission, to a very lost and rebellious and homeless world. In this prayer, Jesus offers his own completed and faithful ministry to the Father in worship. Straightaway he "hands the torch" and prays for the infant community of disciples, "For the same reason that you sent me into the world, I have sent them."

Jesus was sent to be the demonstration of the glory of God in the midst of humankind and to bring the word of eternal life. So now also the church.[3] In this prayer of mission, Jesus moves right on to pray for "those who shall believe" because of the lives and words of this infant community (vss. 20 ff.). Again in John 20:21, Jesus very explicitly tells the disciples and the church, "As the Father has sent me, even so do I send you."

As refounders we dare not miss this point.

Jesus prays and reports his own missional faithfulness, and then the prayer focus shifts to intercession for the ongoing mission of the community of disciples, i.e., the church. This is the reason for the church's very being. It is all so very insistent and germane to our refounding task. It constrains us to look through Christ's eyes at this world in all of its realities. We must love this world and take it as seriously as Jesus did. The fact that this missional identity has become a major area of the church's forgetfulness is a major factor which has brought us to this moment of chaos in the church. Other churches (frequently newer churches), having not forgotten, continue to minister Christ's mission with power and fruitfulness.

Jesus' intercession for this new community is thrilling (John 17). The community and his disciples are to be filled with his very own joy. They are to be formed by his word of truth. Jesus gives them the glory[4] which the Father has given to him. They are to be completely bonded into a oneness-unity such as Father and Son enjoy (restored community). And they are to be filled with, and motivated by, the same love that the Father has for the Son. The reason for all of this? "Those who shall believe in me through their word." All he will do in them is in order to accomplish God's saving mission through them. Jesus does not call the church to be a "custodial" community, but rather to be an obedient and missional people. The tragedy of God's lost and floundering creation is no matter of indifference to the God and Father of our Lord Jesus Christ. And it can never be a matter of indifference to an obedient church.

COFFEE AND DOUGHNUTS ON DECK C

Somehow as the church forgets and devolves into *chaos*, this missionary incarnation of the church gets consigned to a kind of "elective" for a special few, rather than the reason for the whole. Annie Dillard whimsically describes this kind of distressing unreality in the church:

> Why do we people in churches seem like cheerful, brainless tourists on a packaged tour of the Absolute?
>
> The tourists are having coffee and doughnuts on Deck C. Presumably someone is minding the ship, correcting the course, avoiding the icebergs and shoals, fueling the engines, watching the radar screen, noting weather reports radioed in from shore. No one would dream of asking the tourists to do these things. Alas, among the tourists on Deck C, drinking coffee and eating doughnuts, we find the captain, and all the ship's officers, and all the ship's crew. The officers chat; they swear; they wink a bit at slightly raw jokes, just like the regular people. The crew members have funny accents. The wind seems to be picking up.[5]

To seek to *refound* "this old house" in indifference to Christ's compassion for a dark and lost and homeless humankind, would mean becoming a contra-diction, if not an obscenity. Such "churches" existing for themselves and in forgetfulness, become part of the darkness. They become nothing more than "fruitless branches" and religious expressions of the very darkness in which they are called to be light. Such churches are part of the chaos, . . . even if . . . somewhere hidden in them is a dimly burning light that remembers . . .

When Paul, the missionary, wrote to the young church at Corinth, he spoke of the church never again being able to regard men and women as simply mere human persons who could be looked upon with passive indifference. Rather, "the love of Christ leaves us no choice . . . ," he said. We are no longer neutral in this world. When we look at the death of Christ, which rescued us and reconciled us to God, then we are constrained to look *with his love* on those yet to be reached and reconciled to God. This being so, Paul goes right to our missional *raison d'être*—ours is an *ambassadorial appointment*. We are to faithfully tell these same men and women of God's message of reconciliation, and not just tell them, but rather *implore* them to be recon-ciled to God. We do this as God's ambassadors and we do it on behalf of God (cf., 2 Cor. 5: 14 ff. NEB).

The most tragic, the most despicable, the most unlikely scenes of dark-ness and depravity are scenes where God rejoices to work. These are the very settings the church must discern, seek out, and move into in ambassadorial faithfulness. Remember, these are also the very places where the love of God constrains us, . . . and precedes us. The *refounded* church of the twenty-first century will move *toward* the areas of greatest darkness.

Ours is *not* a "packaged tour of the Absolute."

"THE WRATH OF GOD IS BEING REVEALED . . ."

Again, we need to read the first two chapters of Romans. We need to see this catalog of human depravity, not as any legitimation of our contempt for "those other sinners," what with their idolatries, the sexual aberrations, or the wickedness of such men and women. Not at all. The text is not designed as a sterile catalog of the perversity of others (from which we may have been graciously delivered). And certainly we must not look at these chapters as simply an abstract and necessary piece of Paul's theological reasoning (which theology-minded Presbyterians are prone to do). After all, it brings us to the conclusion that whether religious or irreligious, "all have sinned and fall short of the glory of God" (Rom 3:23). This "trashing" of God's "good" creation is met with God's understandable anger.[6]

Rather, we need to look upon these descriptions of eroded humanity as a painful lament over the very tragedy that "sin" is and that it produces. "Total depravity," if those words ever cross our lips, must be used only with tears over the defacing of God's "it is good" creation and glory. The very reality of total depravity drives us on to irresistible grace, to infinite love, to Jesus and his cross, ". . . all are justified freely by his grace through the redemption that is in Christ Jesus" (Rom. 3:24). Such *denouement* drives us to adoration, to thanksgiving, and then necessarily on to costly missionary engagement within this human scene. We are debtors to grace.

As I have already said, *sin* is such an abused word. But it is not an abstraction. Sin is the context in which we live. We need to take time to look at it in our own lives, our own culture, and our own particular (and numerous) subcultures. Sin is a frightening reality which helps us comprehend the tragic context of our daily lives and our neighborhoods.

It is *not neutral* out there!

Understanding this also informs us as to our mission. We need to look at sin's expressions and dimensions with Christ's love for real flesh and blood sinners; we must see these out of his compassionate heart and through his cross.

WAKING UP IN THE TWENTY-FIRST CENTURY:
MISSION INTO THE NEW AND BEWILDERING

I recently woke up from anesthesia after some minor laser surgery. I knew that I wasn't frightened, nor was I in any pain. It was the context that was bewildering. I didn't recognize anything. It took a while for me to orient myself as to who I was, where I was, and what I was doing there. Slowly, as the anesthetic wore off, I began to identify the face of my wife and to acknowledge the friendly medical personnel that came and went. One of the gratuitous emotional realities was that I knew that this immediate state wasn't permanent: I would be discharged, and I would return to a familiar place.

What is different about the Presbyterian Church's present bewilderment is that we *cannot return* to the more identifiable and familiar past. There is indeed a noble and fruitful history behind "this old Reformed house." It is the *cultural context* of our mission that will never again be the familiar one which we have known in our past. It is already radically different. We, as Reformed Christians, can reclaim who we *are*. We can remember and rehearse our great family traditions. We can give thanks for episodes of missionary obedience and fruitfulness. So we can also discern what from our past is useful in our task of *refounding*, and so needs to be reclaimed and recreated. But we can never, never return to "Christendom," when there was a commonly accepted Hebrew-Christian accommodation and ethic in society. Nor can we return to the time when there was an acceptable Christian influence in the affairs of the state and the community. Secularization, or better still *re-paganization*, disdainfully demeans such as *politically incorrect* and dismisses it from the public square.

It is a confusing time. On the cover of Albert Borgman's *Crossing the Postmodern Divide*, there is a picture of the backside of a naked young man sitting on a mountain ridge looking forward (or backward) at distant ridges. In a very challenging philosophical treatise, Borgman spells out the disjuncture between the passing *modern* era and the emerging *postmodern* era. The cover picture becomes all the more poignant as we identify with the one sitting naked between cultural eras. We, too, are trying to make sense out of the changed context in which we live. It is easy for us to identify with him as the *familiar* dissipates and the *unfamiliar* emerges daily with insistent demands and reality.

Douglas Coupland, a *twenty-something generation* author, comes to the end of a somewhat autobiographical book entitled *Life After God*, in which he describes his own generation reared without religion or beliefs or absolutes. He describes the rootlessness and loneliness and disenchantments of his peers. It is a description of life that leaves one feeling sad and empty. Then, as an epilogue, he adds this statement on a page by itself:

Now—here is my secret:

> I tell it to you with an openness of heart that I doubt I shall ever achieve again, so I pray that you are in a quiet room as you hear these words. My secret is that I need God—that I am sick and can no longer make it alone. I need God to help me give, because I no longer seem to be capable of giving; to help me be kind, as I no longer seem capable of kindness; to help me love, as I seem beyond being able to love.[7]

A cry for God! This is a spiritual vacuum which is shared by a generation. This is the failure of the church to communicate to its own children the wonder, the all-encompassing love, and the grace of God for his own creation. Such a poignant cry begins to give us a hint at the challenge before us. It states a first principle of our blueprint for mission as we enter the twenty-first century. It is but one evidence of a bewildering new context for our Presbyterian life and witness. We need to take a deep breath, launch out into some honest searching as to what is out there, and pray for grace of *missional imagination*.

We are all inextricably caught in this transition of cultural paradigms. On one day we go to Blockbuster Video and pick up the video "The Witness" in which Harrison Ford finds refuge from urban crime in the anachronistic Amish farm community in Pennsylvania. He finds caring, stable, and simple folk with a strong sense of communal morality and mutuality. It is most fetching. The nostalgia for such simplicity and security makes us want to go backward and find it. But even the remarkable Amish folk are being sucked further into the vortex of modernity (even as they were in the film). But then, the next day, we go to the same video store and pick up the video "Star Trek: the Next Generation." With the Starship Enterprise we experience a future where time warps, a culture of inter-galactic space travel, and unknown technology confront good and evil in dimensions we have yet to imagine. Captains Kirk, Picard, and their successors live in future centuries, yet they deal with the same mythical confrontations with mysteries, foibles, tragedies, and unknowns that humankind has experienced during its whole history.

WAKE-UP TIME!

Yet the Presbyterian Church has had a very, very difficult time waking up to the future—much less equipping itself for what is inevitably coming down the road. Our confused sense of identity makes us very uncertain how to even begin to respond to a totally strange and new day, much less a new "cultural paradigm."

As we noted in the last chapter, the five-hundred-year *modern* era which began when Columbus opened medieval Europe up to the new world, came dramatically crashing down with the Berlin Wall in 1988. And remember that it is within these historical parameters that the Reformed and Presbyterian witness emerged and in which we have had our history. Here we are now, left standing in the aftermath of both the accomplishments and rubble of modernity. We are left looking at a world that is so much the same and so very different. We are looking still at a world so loved by God. It is strange. We wake into a sense of unreality, yet it is real. It is unexplored new territory. We know we have a history. We are not certain about our future.

However, there may be some good news and some new reality possible here. Many Christians (many Presbyterians) have lived for far too long in a kind of *cultural schizophrenia*. On one hand, we have created a *church world*, a subculture in which we spend a few hours a week. There we talk about things that are perhaps all true, or "spiritual," but which may have little or nothing to do with the other life and the other world in which we live during 160-plus hours of the week—"Coffee and donuts on Deck C!"

Then there is the other world, the *real world*. We have easily compartmental-ized our lives into two worlds, and our *church world* has scarcely affected our other *real world*. The good news is that we are now going to be forced to "get real!" This kind of disjunction[8] (or schizophrenia) has been one of the scandals of the church. It is also one of the fruits of the Enlightenment and of modernity. The *modern* era consigned "religion" to the private world of the individual, but such religion was not acceptable in the public arena. Too many Christians accepted the position that "we don't discuss religion in public." Alas! Such "private religion" has rendered the Christian faith near impotent as any kind of redemptive or transformational force in society. It is also a blatant denial of our incarnational faith.[9] So we have not been able to make the connection between the two worlds.

Our *church world* has been built too much upon a comfortable alliance between church and culture, in which the *real world* says, "You bless us and stay out of the way, and we won't bother you." That alliance is now dissolving around us. We are forced to look with critical eyes on both the true nature of the church as a missional community and the real nature of the world, in its tragic realities, as the context of that mission. This promises some thrilling new missionary understanding of the church. It also promises what Lesslie Newbigin terms, "a missionary confrontation with the world."[10] It has risks. Oh, does it ever have risks. With the redemptive *confrontation* comes the resultant clashes of dominions as well as of minds and wills. Light versus Darkness. These are the dangers we accept along with our missional calling into the everyday world in days ahead. Jesus never tried to hide the reality of this "hatred."

WHAT DOES THE LANDSCAPE OF THE TWENTY-FIRST LOOK LIKE?

The twenty-first century is upon us. What are we looking at? Allow me to walk you into some of the dimensions of challenge to the *refounded-as-a-missional community* Presbyterian Church in the twenty-first century. Let us acknowledge that we will be done with the notion of *comfort-zone custodial congregations*. We will be done with *denominational franchises in posh neighborhoods*. We will renounce *enclaves of yesterday*.

We will be putting our creative imaginations to work around our true identity as communities of Christians who look at our lives and our world through a *Reformed* lens, i.e., through a specific understanding of our Christian faith. We will be spending time reflecting seriously on the "cultural anthropology" of our own neighborhoods, just as overseas missionaries look at the cultural anthropology of the people to whom they are being sent. This will require continual study and fine-tuning. Our whole Christian nurture enterprise will be redirected to take seriously both the command to make disciples, and also the world into which the disciples are sent week by week. Every congregation will become an *intentional missional community*, and every member will be both equipped by and accountable to the community for faithfulness in his or her missionary sojourn.

I want to name seven missional challenges that I see immediately and insistently before the PC(USA). They are: (1) the generational challenge; (2) the urban challenge; (3) the laity and workplace challenge; (4) the "real lost people behind the facade" challenge; (5) the AIDS challenge; (6) the "really poor" challenge; and (7) the challenge of the other religions among us. I want to spend extra time on the first one, the *generational challenge*, and walk through that one into the other six.

1. The Generational Challenge

Most immediately and insistently on our doorstep is the bewilderingly new and different generation of younger adults variously called Generation X, the twenty-something Generation, the Baby Busters, the Alone Generation, or even the Lost Generation. No one person speaks for the whole of this generation, and they spend a lot of time discounting anyone who tries to categorize them. But with these remarkable younger friends, it is not just a classic "growing up" or "old-versus-young" conflict. They are the product of influences and circumstances and cultural forces which make them, on the whole, the first truly *postmodern* and *neo-pagan* generation. Though some Christian parents have taken the time and pains to create Christian cultures in their homes, most have not. This is evident in the fact that Presbyterian youth are leaving the church and not coming back. They are not necessarily going to different kinds of churches, though some are. Rather, they are looking elsewhere for some semblance of structure and meaning to their lives.

It is either exciting or "plumb scary," depending on how you look at it. The Presbyterian Church stands on the threshold of a fruitful and imaginative mission into a new and different culture—or, if it refuses, it is not long for this world (we are always one generation away from extinction). Ignoring this mission will bring about our own blissful demise "in decency and order." We must accept it with all the risks, as an act of missional obedience to a bewilderingly new cultural setting. This *twenty-something* generational culture is the generation born somewhere between 1964 and 1983 (circa). We who are the older generations are being rudely awakened to the first generation formed by media, by postmodern and post-Christian thought patterns, and without a sense of traditions. It is a generation without Hebrew-Christian assumptions, and hence without absolutes (of any kind, moral or otherwise). One of the more obvious evidences of this lack of absolutes is the concept of sexual fulfillment as a normal right, without parameters of right or wrong, and without any particular "big deal" about sexual activity whether heterosexual, homosexual, extramarital, or recreational "making love" (fornication).

It is a generation that has been raised without strong family or neighborhood ties. These young men and women are the product of a 50 percent divorce rate among parents, and a considerable percentage have been sexually abused by their parents. Too many were left alone and essentially neglected by ambitious Baby-Boomer parents seeking their own careers. Intimacy and community are strange concepts.

Add to that an almost universal biblical illiteracy (even among church youth) and a near dismissal ("dissing") of institutional (hence, church and denominational) loyalties. They have been formed by "virtual reality," internet, video games, music such as punk rock (or grunge),[11] despair, cynicism, a lack of much sense of history or future, and anger at the forces which have brought them to this point. They are a generation which has watched the utopian dream of the *eschaton* to be ushered in by technology and human achievement go down in flames (as so much foolishness).

Economically, they live in a very volatile world of instant dot-com millionaires to unemployed wipe-outs. Corporate mergers and bankrupted major players create an uncertainty in the job market. The economy seems momentarily healthy, but the chairman of the Fed warns of recessions and hardships ahead. Stability seems elusive. Even prosperity breeds unsatisfying wealth. Any loyalty to impersonal corporations has vanished in the cubicle world of

Dilbert. All of the creative and entrepreneurial genius of this generation has not brought with it an accompanying sense of *shalom*.

So, what do you have? You have a truly neo-pagan culture of very bright, entrepreneurial, disconnected, and vulnerable young men and women. It is a mission field right in our living rooms. Yet with all of this, a vast spiritual hungering prevails, which is seeking structure and the transcendent, and is undiscerning where it looks for these. The "church" is only a minor blip on the screens of this culture.

The urgency of reaching this generation ought to be alarmingly obvious to the Presbyterian Church, but it doesn't seem to be. If nothing else, the financial implications are stark. Their Baby-Boomer parents (born c. 1945–1963) have been an enigma to the Presbyterian Church. There are libraries of studies on the psyche and character of the Boomers. But the Boomers are an ambivalent generation, with one foot in two cultures, i.e., one in their parents' pre-World War II culture and the other in the demanding new high tech, information-age, consumer-driven culture which they, and we, have created. In the midst of all of this, the Boomers have been more given to divorce and seriatim marriages and to the husband and wife both pursing career goals as the major priority. The Boomers are the quintessential "consumer culture." The victims, of course, are their children. The products of these too-often-dysfunctional homes, absent parents, and "consumerism" lifestyles are the Baby Busters, the now *twenty-something* generation.

Face it, the Boomers are no longer the major issue for the Presbyterian Church. The Boomers are now eligible to join the AARP (American Association of Retired Persons)! They transfer their ambivalence into the church, and so as a generation, the Boomers are ambivalent about Presbyterian institutions, about Reformed tradition, and most certainly about stewardship and congregational disciplines. But get this—the Presbyterian Church is currently financed and supported primarily by the pre-World War II generation (called by some, the Boosters). Business journals estimate that when this older generation passes off the scene (shortly), something into the trillions of dollars in estate money will pass hands to this ambivalent Boomer generation, so that the church will no longer be so confident of financial survival as it has been. The institutional loyalty of the Boomers is not at all to be counted on.

But now here come the Busters, the *twenty-somethings*, who think that Calvin is a cartoon kid who plays with a tiger (or else the first name of jeans worn by sexy bodies). They wonder about a dumb name like "Presbyterian" which, in their popular mind, refers to a bunch of older, stuffy, privileged people who are rather agnostic about their faith and who spend their time in esoteric debates that don't even register on the *twenty-somethings'* scale. Church services are a "big yawn" where the people speak in archaic tongues and refer to the Bible data to which they have never been (consciously) exposed. It's all like an ecclesiastical "Jurassic Park." It simply doesn't communicate.

So the *twenty-somethings* take their spiritual quest elsewhere, frequently into cults and dead-ends.[12] Still, there are churches reaching the *twenty-somethings*— and doing it rather significantly. But they are doing it by creating new forms which are sensitive to the culture, language, and music that communicate to these seekers. These are usually *not* Presbyterian churches, though some are. Some Presbyterian churches, sensitive to the *twenty-something* generation and culture and its heart-cries, have fashioned wonderful and creative alternative/contemporary worship times that have attracted seekers in large numbers (usually pastored by younger men and women who understand).

Still, the resistance is great to such imaginative and creative ministries. "We've always done it this way" is still the working principle of the older and dominant culture (even though in ten to twenty years the older generation will be off the scene and the Busters will be center stage). Beautiful and valid liturgies and music, which spoke meaningfully to other cultures and generations, are assumed to be the "only way" (and God forbid that we should appear informal, human, charismatic, and relational, or that we should question the way our seminaries teach us to do it).

Meanwhile, Calvin continues to play with Hobbes,[13] and the Jurrasic Park Presbyterian Church rumbles along, getting older. Nevertheless, it is clear that time is passing and "the wind seems to be picking up."

The generational challenge of the *twenty-somethings* stands at the threshold of our Presbyterian mission into the twenty-first century. In fifteen or twenty years there could be almost no PC(USA), or a wonderfully different one. Exciting? Scary? Oh yes, but one thing we must never forget is the serendipitous, extravagant, and creative grace of God whose church it is. Frankly, I'm optimistic about the *twenty-somethings*. I think that this *twenty-something* generation is itself a sign of hope. It has a pragmatic, entrepreneurial, realistic, *reforming* capacity which makes me very expectant. These *twenty-somethings*, and those younger, are looking for that "something" that is missing in their culture. They are willing to "look outside the box." Look for awakenings, for surprises. Look for God's "left-handed" and unexpected interventions. Look for a new generation of fresh, tough, streetwise, compassionate, ten-talented biblical and theological leaders with energy and conviction out of this very *twenty-something* culture. But they don't look for more of the same!

I have spent excessive space dealing with this first challenge, because I think it critical. But, much more briefly, I want to pursue the other six challenges that are true of the twenty-first century context into which the *twenty-somethings* will find themselves.

2. The Urban Challenge

There are few challenges more agonizing than the North American cities. For all of the optimistic political and altruistic attempts to bring some hope and beauty back, cities continue to struggle with erosion, poverty, crime, and assorted related ills. Yet here is where the bulk of the population lives. If there is any locus of darkness where the compassion of Christ should look to bring *light* it is these cities. The Presbyterian track record to this point has primarily been one of escape. But there is no longer any escape.

Our cities are, in a very real sense, products of technology. Masses of people with automobiles dash in, work, and then flee to the suburbs, and "cocoon" in their self-contained homes. Half a century ago, C. S. Lewis described hell in the image of "the grey city" where masses lived in close proximity, total loneliness, and non-communication, moving about like so many deaf and mute zombies. Our cities now approximate Lewis' description. Technology has created cities without sidewalks, suburbs that are not neighborhoods, people without community. Someone described the "everywhereness of shopping malls" where crowds go to shop in franchise stores whose owners are a corporation with headquarters half a continent away and where one's identity is not important. Depersonalized life. This loss of community is a tragic dimension of the culture of darkness.

Our *twenty-something* generation will not be able to escape. With the flattening economy, they might just be the generation to reverse "the flight to the suburbs" by which their grandparents and parents escaped. As mission-focused Christians, they might well be the ones to become the urban pioneers, and with *committed communities*,[14] move back into the urban blight to incarnate the gospel of hope and make "the desert blossom like a rose." They may become the *downwardly mobile* and obedient disciples of Jesus Christ who relocate in the areas of greatest need. This could make the *twenty-somethings'* generation one of the exciting missionary generations of church history. But the cities will still be there. They will be there as one of the most needy challenges before us in the twenty-first century. The form of the (Presbyterian) church and its mission strategies may have to change drastically. But, again, the *twenty-something* generation displays a pragmatism and an entrepreneurial gift that makes them uniquely qualified to tackle this. And remember—church history proves that it is in just such unlikely areas of darkness that God has a surprising way of showing forth (or breaking forth in) his new creation. The *refounded*

Presbyterian church will have to take cities seriously and respond to the heart of God for their welfare. And that is a daunting and an exciting prospect.

3. The Laity and the Workplace Challenge

There is a smoldering and quiet rebellion going on by the 95-plus percent of the church who are God's λαος, the laity. They are more and more unac-cepting of a "clergy-focused" church, whose agenda is built by "church professionals" who are apparently indifferent to the 165 hours that laity spend in homes and workplaces. Especially workplaces. It is during these 165 hours of being the "church scattered" that God's people are most truly the salt of the earth, most uniquely "the church." It is with family, neighbors, fellow citi-zens, and working colleagues that they are involved in being *God's missionary incarnation*. This is a tough place to be. It is here that ethical challenges, ideo-logical conflicts, practical problems, personalitiy differences, uses of influence, alien values, and intrusions are most intense. The dismal effect of the church on American society in recent decades, for all of its noise, is attributable to this indifference about equipping men and women for their ministry in the workplace.

In the twentieth century, the church all but avoided this. It was not a part of the Presbyterian Church's agenda. To be an "outstanding layperson" has been to serve on congregational or denominational committees and councils, or to become involved in church programs, and, of course, contribute gener-ously to the budget. The laity are hardly in view in the theological education in given seminaries. Tim Dearborn did a study of this phenomenon under a Murdock Trust grant. He writes

> Lay persons feel under-valued and under-equipped. I have interviewed over 150 lay persons from various occupations over the past three years. More than 90% indicated that they have never received any significant support, guid-ance or even interest regarding their jobs from their pastor. The church is more interested in their volunteer time than in their occupations. Their jobs are validated as means to other ends: income to contribute to Christian causes, places of evangelism, ways to deepen the credibility of the Church. Few find from their church significant support or guidance on integrating their work into their faith, and in addressing the complex ethical, economic and leadership issues they face at work with the resources of the gospel.[15]

Or again, when Dearborn gathered together a group of seminary deans and faculty with clergy and laypersons, they collated what would be the ten highest priority areas in which clergy needed to be equipped. When they had come up with their profile, it was noted that few, if any, of these courses are currently required as foundational in most seminaries. In other words, the church is equipping its leadership for a role that nobody is asking for, or for a church that is not there.[16]

Already, my *twenty-something* friends are looking at that one with determination in their eyes and saying to the church, "Get real!" The *refounded* Presbyterian Church will be focused on equipping the laity for ministry in the workplace and in a real world. The focus will *not* be on the clergy. The "clergy" of the twenty-first century will be totally redefined, as will the whole concept of theological education. Count on it!

4. The Challenge of Real Lost Persons Behind the Facade

Because I see exciting hope in the *twenty-something* generation, I also believe that it is going to be much less provincial and judgmental about all the persons out there (outside of the church) who, to use the term, aren't "church types." But neither will they be willing to abandon these persons to their darkness. Compassion conveys real *gut-level* feelings for a person or situation. Jesus is our model as he had compassion for those suffering in darkness and helplessness. The *refounded* Presbyterian Church, as inhabited by *twenty-somethings*, is going to have eyes for all those folk who are "lonely in the world since God died," or however you express the homelessness of those without God and without hope in the world (Eph. 2:12).

There are all of those folk whom we meet in the factory, office, hospital, neighborhood, or on the campus, who put up good fronts. But behind the facades, they are living in their own personal hell. It may be a facade of adolescent shenanigans and reckless sexuality, arrogant wealth and power, smug success and its accompanying hedonism, lofty and condescending intellectual hubris, social and racial elitism, street gangs, compulsive altruism, drug and substance abuse, corporate greed and individual complicity in it, "consumerism," "hot button" agendas and crusades (abortion rights, law and order, etc.), or pathological surfing the internet. But whatever the facade, there lies underneath the common roots of the fact that men and women apart from the Creator God have a void that only God can fill. They are "lost in the cosmos."[17]

If they are lonely in the world because "God has died," it may get lonelier still. Which makes it all the more critical that a missional focused Presbyterian Church is going to be "a friend of sinners," and like its Savior, will be seeking and rescuing such. The *refounded* Presbyterian Church will see its communal life as part of that good news of God and have a large "Welcome" mat out for God's returning sons and daughters.

5. The Challenge of AIDS

"Where the darkness is the greatest," . . . yes, and there is no more distressing challenge than that of AIDS, whether its victims are profligate and sexually irresponsible, whether they are unwitting victims of blood transfusions, or whether they are the children of AIDS carriers. The church of the twenty-first century, including individual congregations, are going to have to look this one right in the eye and look with compassion. From the words of scripture come the words of Jesus, "Blessed are the merciful, for they shall receive mercy."

The loneliness and stigma of AIDS victims is one costly place where the compassion of Christ becomes *our mission*. This means that there will also need to be a coming to grips with those of sexual lifestyles and homosexuality, which our church finds falling short of God's purpose for human sexuality. All the same, the darkness becomes the place where the light must shine and where sinners are heartily welcomed. Enough said! The challenge is inescapable to an obedient mission community.

6. The Challenge of the "Really Poor"

Our economy has created an underclass of poor people, cut off from resources of real help, who live in a sort of hopeless despair that is tragic. The politics of these days rewards wealth and forsakes the helpless poor to their own "bootstraps." But if one is going to be formed by the narrative of scripture and conformed to the image of Christ, such indifference is a total contradiction. Yet the Presbyterian Church has been a middle-class phenomenon, insulated from such real poverty, except in patronizing acts or guilt-motivated altruism.

I'm not sure that my own generation (Boosters), or the Boomers, will be able to break out of this middle-class bondage and disobedience to Christ. But here again, I am hopeful for the *twenty-something* generation. Conservative and middle-class Presbyterians beat-up on *liberation theology* (considered a dirty word). But it doesn't help any. Jesus inaugurated his ministry with an announcement of good news to the poor (Luke 4:18) and assured John's disciples that he had fulfilled one of the messianic signs by preaching good news to the poor (Luke 7:24). Those in prison in the Gospels were in prison because of debts. Apart from some Latin Americans getting this theology tangled up with a Marxist solution, there is no question that in the Bible, God displays a special compassion or a "preferential option" for the poor. In the telling passage in Matthew 25 where the day of judgment is portrayed, those who are compassionate and caring for the homeless (strangers), hungry, thirsty, naked, sick, and imprisoned are those who receive Christ's words "Come, blessed of my Father."

But the *refounded* Presbyterian Church cannot acknowledge this from afar. Our gospel is *incarnational* through and through. As Jesus took on flesh and blood and dwelt among us, so the church must "relocate among the poor," with a message of reconciliation to God and neighbor, with the sharing of lives, skills, and resources that will enable the poor toward self-sufficiency. The church must learn from the poor neighbors some very profound lessons in humanity.

7. The Challenge of Other Religions Among Us

And finally, the *refounded* church, like any good missionary going cross-culturally, is going to have to see in other religions the quest of the human heart for transcendence, for meaning, for its true home—for God. Islam is no longer halfway across the world. The mosque is around the corner. Buddhist temples likewise. My own little neighborhood has folk from most major national groups and from many religions. And, of course, there are those people who are burned out on religion and take yet another religion, namely "secularism," which in itself is a religion, or a "faith position" in no god at all.

Why, again, do folk take up with such a shadowy religious philosophy as New Age? Why the interest in the occult? Why the resurgence of Eastern religions such as Buddhism and Hinduism?

My missionary heart has to believe that all of these are legitimate searches for God that fall short. They all contain some very commendable attributes, as well as some tragic blank spots. But folk who adhere to these religions are now our neighbors, and we in the church need to be in a position to intelligently hold conversation with these in a sensitive and caring kind of evangelistic dialogue. We have things to learn. We also have a word of hope from God in Christ to share.

The equipping of a missionally-focused Presbyterian Church will make the understanding of, and thoughtful conversation with, these religions (and lack thereof) a part of our equipping ministry among God's people. The late Presbyterian missionary William McElwee Miller went to Iran (then Persia) as a young man and walked the length of that sizable nation, preaching the gospel and getting to know the people in every village along the way. He spent a long career there in loving conversation with the Islamic folk, demonstrating to them the love of Christ and quietly telling them of the reasons for his faith in Jesus. There is now a second and third generation of Iranian people who have come to know Christ through that loving ministry. And now that kind of context exists in our cities and neighborhoods; that kind of ministry becomes our mission. Our neighbors become our ministry.

And this is the culture of the twenty-first century, in which the Presbyterian Church, *refounded*, will obey, bear fruit, and flourish under God's grace and empowering—or, in which it will become a relic of history and a monument to missional indifference and insensitivity, its lamp removed from the lampstand.

BEYOND CHAOS: HOPE AND NEW CREATION

Having now used the word *chaos* frequently, let me invite you to stop and ponder that this isn't really a bad thing. Ponder the reality that it is usually only out of *chaos* that new expressions of ministry can come. The rigid structural forms with which the PC(USA) lived in the twentieth century are rapidly devolving into *chaos*, and that very reality is what should give us hope for a truly *refounded* Reformed house within the "one holy catholic and apostolic church." In the twenty-first century, the boundaries of such traditions will not be at all rigid, but rather the boundaries will vary and traditions will network and share gifts in common mission. There will be open doors between vital Christian traditions, and Christians will move easily between them. But the presence of the Reformed witness will be an essential element of the flavor of Christ's church. What has now faded into too much obscurity will again, with dynamism, come to "reflect a particular stance within the history of God's people."[18]

Yes! Christ's church never dies. Particular expressions of it do. But the Spirit breathes life, and some new expression, form, or ministry emerges with life and worship, and the work goes on. I would not be surprised if many of our eleven thousand Presbyterian congregations were to choose death, . . . and they will find it. There will be considerable church real estate on the market in the next fifty years. But many Reformed communities will come together in worship, meet with the God of their salvation, and determine to "lose their lives for Christ's sake and the gospel's." The Breath of God will energize them to *refound* their life together, link up with other such congregations, and become once again a very bright and shining light in a very dark world. God always has a future and a hope for those who trust him.

Out of the present denominational *chaos* emerges our very hope for some radical *refounding* of "this old Reformed house."

So now we turn to the previous and all-important issue—Jesus Christ. We need to look now at the *flip side* of ". . . even so do I send you," which is, "As the Father has sent me . . ." Our design at refounding must proceed out of "*Sheer devotion to Christ.*"

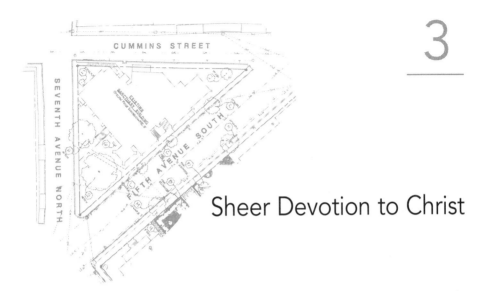

3

Sheer Devotion to Christ

WHAT I WANT TO SAY HERE, I DARE NOT SAY LIGHTLY, OR WITHOUT my reader's full attention. It is the most critical point in all of our project of *refounding*. It sounds so obvious that it might easily be dismissed with a cursory "Of course!" But it is *the* critical point in the church's essence. So listen very carefully—If Jesus gave us our mission, with his words: ". . . *even so do I send you*,". . . *then* Jesus himself is the mission: "*As the Father has sent me*, . . ." (John 20:21).

Who is this incredible figure? Where did he come from? Why did he come? What did he do? What did he teach? What did he say about himself? What does he say about us? What promises does he give? What demands does he make? Is he God? Is he human? What is there in him that makes all of this so very insistent and inescapable? Is this Jesus indeed the *Lord*? Is he the Lord who calls forth our worship and adoration?

The living church's answer? An unequivocal "Yes and Amen!"[1]

Is this not obvious? It would seem to be. But, again, the *Laodacean pathology* intrudes itself so quickly. A church begins well, built upon Jesus Christ. It never consciously forsakes him or disbelieves him. However, in its institutional life, it drifts into other priorities and agendas, and *Christ the center* is ever so unconsciously (inadvertently? unintentionally?) moved, little by little, to the margins, and then finally outside the door. *Christ-the-taken-for-granted*, patiently knocking and seeking to enter again and to sit at table with those who bear his name (Rev. 3:20). Jesus becomes the *outsider* to his own. They and we take that dear one for granted, and consign him to the status of an observer from the outside. Institutional life is flourishing. The budget is balanced and there is money to spare. The institution is thoroughly self-sufficient. It rejoices in its success and growth. With its mind, it still believes in Jesus. But its heart is elsewhere.

Jesus sadly rebukes such a church. It is nauseous and is not to be taken seriously—"I will spit you out." But Jesus' heart still loves and longs for this pitiable, *successful* congregation; "To him who [gets over this pathology], I will give the right to sit with me on my throne, just as I overcame and sat down with my Father on his throne" (Rev. 3:21).

What is the cure? The cure begins with earnest repentance (3:19), or perhaps more correctly, with a broken heart. It begins with acknowledging the pathology of presuming upon Christ. It begins with our turning to a disciplined, intentional, and intense focus on Jesus. It begins with the primary place of *adoration*. Those of us who are the Presbyterian Church (and the whole catholic church) must cease being timid, muted, or embarrassed about Jesus. We must get beyond bland and mindless devotional thoughts about him and his purpose for all of creation. If the mission to which he sends us is his design for this church's existence, then he himself is the only true foundation.

It is more than folly—it is a travesty—to even begin to think about *refounding* this Reformed and Presbyterian "old house" for the twenty-first century apart from our determined conviction that the only true foundation is Jesus Christ. He only must be our joy, our focus, our heart's desire, and the one before whom we deliberately bow and name Savior and Lord of the church (as well as our individual Savior and God). The *refounded* Presbyterian Church must begin the rebuilding by being deliberately *Christ-o-centric* through and through, by being "lost in wonder, love, and praise."

Nothing else matters. *Christ* is where it begins. Everything else must flow out of this adoration of the Son of God—Jesus, name above all names. In recent missions studies, missionary historians have been overwhelmed with the astounding evangelizing impact of the Irish and Anglo-Saxon monastic communities in the time c. 500–700 C.E. They were a key to the evangelizing of the whole of Europe, and yet they were so very poor. These worshipers lived on the margins of existence. What the historians have discovered is very simple, and it is totally germane to our quest here. These monastics accomplished such amazing feats with nothing but *their sheer devotion to Christ*. It is this devotion to Christ which must be the motivation for any attempt to *refound* the Presbyterian and Reformed witness for the twenty-first century.

QUESTION: DO WE PRESBYTERIANS
REALLY WANT THE JESUS OF SCRIPTURES?

It is one thing to establish the Christ-o-centric fact of scriptures, but then again, who are we talking about? There is something quite enigmatic in that the church which professes Christ as Lord is so very much like the culture around it. Something is awry here. Do we Presbyterian folk really want the Herald of the Messianic Kingdom (kingdom of God)? Do we want the sovereign Lord who has come to create all things new? Do we want the one who is the demonstration of the New Creation? Do we want one who does not play games with the Law and the Prophets (i.e., the Old Testament), but rather insists that he did not come to abolish these but to fulfill them through and through? Do we want one who claims that to see *him* is to see the Father, that to hear *his words* is to hear the Father's words, and that to see *his works* is to see the Father's works?

It is axiomatic in C. S. Lewis' *Chronicles of Narnia*, that Aslan (the Christ figure in the stories) is not "a *tame* Lion."[2] If we come to Jesus expecting a "tame" or "safe" religious figure, we are in for a great surprise. Jesus defies human description or categories. There is a holy unpredictability about him and yet an infinite goodness and faithfulness which are his nature. It is, again, something of an axiom in Narnia that the longer you look at Aslan, the bigger he gets. So it is as we gaze upon Jesus Christ! For starts, the overwhelming image is that the sovereign and transcendent Creator God has appeared in human form. Who would have thought?

JESUS: THE FOCUS OF THE NEW TESTAMENT

How can one be so dogmatic about this? It is really quite simple. One has only to look at the inescapable focus of all of the New Testament documents. Begin with two images having to do with foundations. The first is that of Jesus' own teaching, that the person who builds the permanent house is the one who "hears these words of mine and puts them into practice" (Matt. 7:24). Such is the solid rock upon which foundations are laid. Jesus' teachings in the Sermon on the Mount, and his other sermons, are to be heard and practiced. The salt is to be good salt, the light is to shine unhindered, and the kingdom behavior is to be visible to humankind. Idle profession without practice is disastrous. Note, too, that previous to this "house on the rock" image is the searching passage (Matt. 7:21–23) which states that mere orthodox theological propositions are not the ultimate test ("Lord, Lord"), nor are ecclesiastical or spiritual busy works done in Jesus' name. It is those whom Jesus *knows*, whose lives flow out of a relationship of knowledge and love and response to him. Such lives in living relationship to Jesus both know him and his teachings, and continue to do his work. Such are the bearers of the fruit of the New Creation. This passage probes the mystery of our oneness with Christ, but it unmistakably describes how the life that embraces Jesus by faith is embraced by him, and then demonstrates Christ to the world. This is the life built on the rock!

The other image is the apostle Paul's; "For no one can lay any foundation other that the one already laid, which is Jesus Christ" (1 Cor. 3:11); and, ". . . God's household, built upon the foundation of the apostles and prophets, with Christ Jesus himself as the chief cornerstone" (Eph. 2:20). Paul is jealous that no one build any kind of ecclesiastical structure on a foundation that is incompatible with the church being the sacred temple of God—the dwelling place of God by the Holy Spirit. Paul has already acknowledged that our Christian enterprise is totally foolish to the "wisdom of this age." Such a statement is somehow ominous to our current frenzied quest for the "successful church." It is also incompatible with the church that is designed by the current *zeitgeists*, or the standards of this age. When this foundation is absent, the building becomes antithetical to the mission of Christ.

There is a consistency in the many metaphors in the New Testament. They are all focused in Christ. Jesus told his followers at Caesarea Philippi that upon Peter's affirmation that "Jesus is the Messiah," he would call forth and build an assembly of the dominion of God. Paul calls this same assembly "the body of Christ." Paul goes even further and states that by the power (i.e., the Holy Spirit) at work in and among Jesus' people, the church would be the expression of the glory of God, even as Christ is the expression of the glory of God (Eph. 3:21).

Every New Testament document begins with its affirmation of focus on Jesus Christ and of the centrality of Christ. The gospels are all self-consciously records of all the events surrounding the birth, life, works, teachings, death, and resurrection of Christ. Acts, by Luke's account, is a record of the continuation of the works of Christ in his new community of followers. Paul's letters frequently begin with hymns of sheer adoration of Christ. Paul states that his preaching is focused in the preaching of Christ crucified, however foolish that sounds to the dominant social order (1 Cor. 1:23).

(Jesus) is the image of the invisible God, the firstborn over all creation. For by him all things were created: things in heaven and on earth, visible and invisible, whether thrones or powers or rulers or authorities: all things were created by him and for him. He is before all things, and in him all things hold together.

And he is the head of the body, the church; he is the beginning and the first-born from among the dead, so that in everything he might have the supremacy. For God was pleased to have all his fullness dwell in him, and through him to reconcile to himself all things, whether things on earth or things in heaven, by making peace through his blood, shed on the cross (Col. 1:15–20).

Is that an awesome statement or what? Words are just totally inadequate to bear such weight of glory. How does one read through that without being overwhelmed? Do you shout in ecstasy? Dance for joy? Fall on your face in adoration? Lay your hand upon your mouth? Everything else seems trivial by comparison.

Then there is the prologue to Hebrews:

In the past God spoke to our forefathers through the prophets at many times and in various ways, but in these last days he has spoken to us by his Son, whom he appointed heir of all things, and through whom he made the universe. The Son is the radiance of God's glory and the exact representation of his being, sustaining all things by his powerful word. After he had provided purification for our sins, he sat down at the right hand of the Majesty in heaven (Heb. 1:1–3).

All of which is to underscore the fact that it is not at all coincidental that our first ordination vow as Presbyterian leaders asks of us,

Do you trust in Jesus Christ your Savior, acknowledge him Lord of all and Head of the Church, and through him believe in one God, Father, Son, and Holy Spirit? (*Book of Order,* G–14.0207a)

This forthright question asks us to identify wholeheartedly, mentally and morally, with the Church's faith in Jesus as our (both personal and corporate) Savior, our Lord, and the acknowledged Head of his Church (in the context of our Trinitarian faith). It is when this ultimate reality of Christ and devotion to him grows dim in the church's consciousness, or becomes perfunctory, that *chaos* begins to appear.

And this happens with frightening regularity in the history of the church. In the first century, it already appears in several of the churches in Asia Minor (Rev. 2–3). The *Laodacean pathology* was so subtle. Founded directly or indirectly by the apostles, our sister congregation in Laodacea already had created a corporate life that became so preoccupied with itself that Christ was unconscionably left outside the door, seeking entrance. I'm quite certain that if you had asked anyone in the Laodacean congregation where Christ was, they would have professed his present importance to them. Or if you asked whether they had forgotten Christ, they would have been vigorous in denial. They weren't denying Christ, it was only that he was no longer the one central, formative, and all-consuming reality in their individual and corporate life.

It happens so subtly. Infinite in patience, Christ knocks on the door and asks to be allowed back in to sit at the table and to be at the heart of the church's life once again (as he does at our Presbyterian door). He even promises that if we overcome this preoccupation with prosperity and a comfortable life and invite him back in, he will cause us to sit with him on his Father's throne.

It is almost as if our institutional preoccupation and our apparent focus on survival have drugged us into an amnesia about Jesus. We run merrily along for long stretches without reference to that one who is Alpha and Omega of all things. How can that be? It is reminiscent of the episode in C. S. Lewis' *The Silver Chair* (part of the series *Chronicles of Narnia*), when Jill, Scrubb, and Puddleglum had been sent into the underworld by the lion Aslan to find a long lost prince of Narnia. The prince, it turns out, is captive to the sorcery of the seductive, deceptive, and evil Green Witch (who, when crossed, quickly changes into a malicious giant green serpent). There comes a point when the Green Witch, through a narcotic smoke from some magic green powder thrown into the fireplace, along with the hypnosis of music and distortion of words, tries to remove from their memories any recollection of the lion Aslan or of the land of Narnia. Slowly the sorcery and the hypnotic brainwash begin to take effect, making them forget and doubt. They were losing the clear memory of who they were, why Aslan had sent them, and even of the reality of Narnia. The brave and comical "Marshwiggle" Puddleglum turns the tide.

> The Prince and the two children were standing with their heads hung down, their cheeks flushed, their eyes half closed; the strength all gone from them; the enchantment almost complete. But Puddleglum, desperately gathering all his strength, walked over to the fire. Then he did a very brave thing. He knew it wouldn't hurt him quite as much as it would hurt a human, for his feet (which were bare) were webbed and hard and cold-blooded like a duck's. But he knew it would hurt him badly enough; and so it did. With his bare foot he stamped on the fire, grinding a large part of it into ashes on the flat hearth. And three things happened all at once. . . .[3]

The spell was broken, the witch was exposed for what she was, and everyone's head was cleared. Aslan and Narnia became the central focus of their lives once more. Then the redemptive solution to the story emerges.

So with the PC(USA). Too often we have been drugged by a culture that has popularized Jesus, until the biblical message is very dim in our corporate consciousness and in the church's missional calling. The popular mind of the church is seduced by—and lives content with—a partial, romanticized, and truncated image of Jesus. Any suggestion otherwise draws puzzled looks, as though one were suggesting something wholly alien to the church's faith. But if we were to shake off our dullness and forgetfulness and focus again on knowing Jesus Christ, trusting his saving work, and giving ourselves to the observance of all that he commanded (cf., Matt. 28:20), as well as holy obedience to his mission mandate, the future would be very, very bright indeed for this Reformed "old house."

But right there we come upon a major dilemma. In North American culture, and in the understanding of a sizable part of the church, Jesus has been so reduced, truncated, romanticized, or perceived as part of the "self-fulfillment" ethos, that we have a very difficult time understanding what he is about or what we are to be about.

WHO IS JESUS? AND WHAT IS THE GRAND DESIGN?

It's not all as easy as it sounds, however. I'm uncomfortable with so much that passes for New Testament Christianity in our popular culture. There's something that comes across in all too much of the information about Jesus and the Christian faith that somehow leaves out key pieces to the biblical concept of *salvation*, and in so doing, leaves many of my *twenty-something* friends more confused by it all. Remember, we are now in a very real *neo-pagan* and *post-Christian* (not to mention *postmodern*) culture. All of the "Jesus talk" and the "church talk" that appear in the media are so out of context (not to mention off the wall) and refer to such unknown references, that increasingly the most elemental data of the New Testament are totally obscure to the younger populace. Add to that the grotesque distortions that the secular media love to hang on the slightest aberration within the Christian community, and you have a setting that is reminiscent of Paul talking to the Athenians and the Corinthians, i.e., non-comprehension.

There is no false reverence or feigned piety with my younger friends. One of them put it to me bluntly, asking "Who's this Jesus guy you talk about? What's he all about? What's the big deal with him?"

I think those are very, very good questions, and now we can come at it fresh, which we need to do. As I write this chapter, it is the season of Advent and Christmas. Sentiment hears all of the familiar Advent texts and they sound "right." But stand back from the overly familiar and look at the juxtaposition of the prophetic texts from Isaiah from several centuries before the advent of Christ, with the Revelation texts from several decades after the advent. They speak of God's grand design in terms that are cosmic and all-encompassing, and that take place with certainty right in the midst of the economic, political, historical, conflict-ridden realities of this human scene.

> The Lord will lay bare his holy arm in the sight of all the nations, and all the ends of the earth will see the salvation of our God (Isa. 52:10).

> And he will be called Wonderful Counselor, Mighty God, Everlasting Father, Prince of Peace. Of the increase of his government and peace there will be no end. He will reign on David's throne and over his kingdom, establishing and upholding it with justice and righteousness from that time on and forever. The zeal of the Lord Almighty will accomplish this (Isa. 9:7).

Does that sound somewhat familiar? Is it for real? Is God really up to this? Well, look at the other end of things.

> The kingdom of the world has become the kingdom of our Lord and of his Christ, and he will reign for ever and ever (Rev. 11:15).

> Now have come the salvation and the power and the kingdom of our God, and the authority of his Christ (Rev. 12:10a).

> You are worthy, our Lord and God, to receive glory and honor and power, for you created all things, and by your will they were created and have their being (Rev. 4:11).

> I did not see a temple in the city, because the Lord God Almighty and the Lamb are its temple. . . . The nations will walk by its light, and the kings of the earth will bring their splendor (Rev. 21:22, 24).

And as if that didn't give us some clues to some grand design, then look again at what the angel Gabriel says to the unsuspecting Mary.

> Greetings, you who are highly favored! The Lord is with you. . . . Do not be afraid, Mary, you have found favor with God. You will be with child and give birth to a son, and you are to give him the name Jesus. He will be great and will be called the Son of the Most High. The Lord God will give him the throne of his father David, and he will reign over the house of Jacob forever; his kingdom will never end (Luke 1:28, 30–33).

It all sounds rather grand and even grandiose. But what we get in the gospel accounts is not at all grandiose. It is, rather, the record of a peasant living on the margins of the Roman empire and saying outrageous things about being "one with the Father God," or that anyone "who has seen me has seen the Father God." Come on, now. Get real. Jesus moves among marginal people who have real misunderstandings and human infirmities, and he does it with gentleness. He eschews the religious trappings of the religious leaders. He does supernatural things like opening blind eyes and raising the dead. At the same time, he isn't interested in popular acclaim. He talks of a new dominion of God and teaches radical principles. Then he escapes the crowds who want to install him as leader and goes off with a few and prays. The whole picture of Jesus doesn't seem to compute.

All the while, he *is* announcing a new *kingdom*. As a matter of fact, he is not even subtle in letting it be known that all of that prophetic hope of a *messiah*, of which Isaiah wrote, is unfolding right before their eyes—good news to the poor; sight to the blind; release for the debtor prisoners; cleansing and healing of lepers; hearing restored to the deaf; and the dead raised to life (cf., Isa. 61:1–2; 35:5–6).

JESUS REDEFINES EVERYTHING

When Jesus went public in his ministry, he had one dominant theme—The kingdom of God is at the doorstep. Get your priorities straight and believe God's good news! (Mark 1:15). The not-so-subtle inference is, of course, that the kingdom is at the doorstep in this very preacher, Jesus. There is a whole lot of contemporary uneasiness about the word "kingdom" and its contemporary meaninglessness. But the problem is not a matter of meaningless so much as it is of a redefined concept of "king" or of rule and dominion. What the church has missed (at least as early as the fourth century) and continues to miss is that *Jesus radically and fundamentally redefined the whole concept of king and kingdom, of authority and dominion, of lordship and greatness.*

More than that, he demonstrates in himself his own redefinition. "See, your king comes to you, gentle and riding on a donkey," (Matt. 21:5); or from the brilliant imagery of Revelation, "See, the Lion of the tribe of Judah, the Root of David, has triumphed. . . . Then I saw a Lamb, looking as if it had been slain, standing in the center of the throne, . . ."(Rev. 5:5–6); or, "For who is greater, the one who is at table, or the one who serves? Is it not the one who is at the table? But I am among you as one who serves" (Luke 22:27).

Though there was an aura of mystery and power all around Jesus, it was present in the *ordinariness* of a peasant, a very real human being who insisted on the servant role. Oh, there is no question that Jesus was also divine. He said so.

"Anyone who has seen me has seen the Father" (John 14:9). "I and the Father are one" (John 10:30). He had divine foreknowledge of the cross and resurrection. But look closer—the sovereign Lord of the universe chose as his point of entry a peasant family in a marginal nation—with all of the inconveniences of being a long way from home, without influence, without even a place to stay. The point of entry was the uterus of a young girl and the helplessness of an infant.

Why? Why not come with the human concepts of importance and why not a display of grandness and worthiness? Splendor, trumpets, attendants, public acclaim. Why not? Because all is such a fundamental misunderstanding of the glory of God, of true greatness, and of the nature of true authority. It is all exaltation at the expense of others and indifference to the "least of these."

Yes, Jesus fundamentally and radically redefines everything . . . *everything*! God, humankind, sin, relationships, authority, nature, meaning, power, success, blessedness, . . . *everything*. This is the Jesus that the church needs to look at afresh. Just stop and think—given our essential presupposition of the sovereign, transcendent Creator-God, the God who is God—and one has to ask, Why in the world did God choose to pull off this whole *muted Jesus* episode as his way of revealing his glory to humankind? How in the world does God demonstrate who he is? How he thinks? What his will and good purpose is in it all? How he looks upon humankind? How does he come to grip with its foibles, rebellion, arrogance, tragedy, and lostness?

What you come up with doesn't fit any of our "normal" human categories. New Testament documents give us a portrait, and it doesn't fit our human concepts of anything, especially of God, power, glory, and majesty. The God of gods makes his entrance into the human scene by a back door and in near silence. God as a human being. Oh, to be sure, there are some unusual events recorded surrounding his birth. The godly old Simeon, one of the few to recognize the birth's significance, states that "For my eyes have seen your salvation which you have prepared in the sight of all people, a light for the revelation to the Gentiles and the glory to your people Israel" (Luke 2:30–32). Then a somewhat normal childhood occurs in silence. Not much is said.

Then Jesus goes public as a mature adult, and we have records of the two to three years of his career with a handful of intimate disciples and of his teachings. These records contain some unsafe, untame teachings, namely that

1. In himself, the manifestation of the reign of Yahweh is at the threshold (Question: What is this kingdom of God and how is it intruding? Get real);
2. In himself, the Law/Torah is not superseded but is given new intensity and is fulfilled; he, himself, is the fulfillment and more—relationship with God and with humankind;

3. At the heart of his mission from the Father is to be rejected and executed in shame, . . . but that cross will be followed by resurrection.

Slowly it begins to dawn on us that Jesus is not defining anything of significance in any way such as we, or anybody else, would do. God is not glorifying or revealing himself according to our definitions or categories. Again, Jesus is fundamentally and radically redefining God, humankind, sin, success, power, glory, and greatness—and somehow we're not getting it. His cross is at the heart of this redefinition. He concludes this advent in a controversial but muted departure (Ascension Day doesn't get much press). This *redefinition* is the very reason that it is all "foolishness" to the world. Jesus stands all of the ordinary human goals and definitions "on their head." For instance,

- Sin is not some dismal, life-cramping or guilt-generating list of things that an ominous judge is snooping out in order to make us miserable. Rather, sin is simply missing the whole point of our creation and the true ecstasy of belonging to God;
- "Self-fulfillment" is a big "*not*." The frenzied quest for self-fulfillment makes God utilitarian to my self interest. And it doesn't work;
- Oddly enough, true and profound life is found in (would you believe?) self-denial. Success is losing one's life for the sake of Jesus and the gospel;
- Weakness is strength;
- Servanthood is greatness;
- Wealth is poverty and vice-versa;
- Acceptance is rejection;
- Intimacy with the Creator-God comes by his invitation into Christ's "upside-down" life;
- And, "blessedness" (profound happiness) is found in identity with the poor, merciful living, seeking peace, hungering for justice and righteousness, and even in suffering and being reviled and persecuted for righteousness' sake.

Well, Jesus' "upside-down"[4] life was far too much for both the Roman occupying government and the Jewish temple establishment. They, wedded to their human definitions, found him not only troublesome, but a bit loony and dangerous. So these two human powers colluded together, exercising their prerogative to destroy him. *But*, . . . their very act of execution became the most upside-down of all, because God used their scaffold to become the altar upon which the eternal sacrifice was made to reconcile the world to God; true power was radically redefined. Christ's weakness and death became true power and true life. Rome and Jerusalem apparently won, but they *lost* ultimately. Jesus appeared to have lost to them, but in so "losing" he "disarmed the powers and authorities, . . . made a public spectacle of them, triumphing over them by the cross" (Col. 2:15).

Such a redefinition has awesome implications. Think for instance of something which can be so easily discounted by mere humans like *prayer*. Prayer takes on enormous potential. P. T. Forsyth says that prayer "has more effect on history than civilization has."[5] The messages of the cross, the kingdom of God, the New Creation, and Eternal Life all bespeak the same reality. They all make known the reality of the sovereign God coming to make all things new in Jesus Christ. The preaching of this message is such foolishness by human definition. So also the act of our praying is foolishness. The dominion of God is, likewise, foolishness to our merely human society. John Perkins calls this upside-down kingdom "the quiet revolution." It simply doesn't play by the same rules as the dominions of this world with the plausibility structures thereof. It is like leaven, which quietly but irresistibly permeates the whole loaf of dough. This radically redefined kingdom, however, is redemptive, creative, sensitive to the human tragedy, and quite willing to "die" to all the prerequisites of success and prominence for the sake of the Servant King (cf. Rom. 6).

REFOUNDING AND REDEFINITION

To be faithful to Jesus, one (or the church) must absorb his or her message of the New Creation (i.e., the kingdom of God) with its *small gate* of repentance, its *narrow way* of discipleship, and its *inner principles* of life formed by a new reality. It has demands and costs and motivation . . . all of which are alien and often despised by the dominion of darkness from which we are delivered. True blessedness (or however one describes life as it is intended to be, life which has found its true home) comes from the exact opposite direction than that from which all of the self-help, self-fulfillment, "how-to" books of our own culture seek it. Self-denial, servanthood, losing one's life for Christ's sake and the gospels, a daily dying (i.e., taking up the cross) to the working principles of this age are Christ's invitations. These all seem so abysmally negative to this age, and yet they are the "foolishness" that is the doorway to the "beyond asking or imagining" reality of the life of God. And it is a life that experiences an ever expanding love and joy as one lives by its principles. But, . . . the *door* is Jesus. And Jesus grows in our understanding the longer we focus on him in adoration.

Jesus' birth *began* this redefinition. After all, "Glory to God in the highest" [translate: the highest revelation of God] spoken to a bunch of minimum wage farm hands out back is not too humanly convincing. And the statement to Mary that the child she was carrying would sit upon the throne of his father David, and that his kingdom would have no end leaves the skeptic a bit incredulous, doesn't it? But the very redefinition is both *demonstrated and explicated* in Jesus' life and teachings. His death and resurrection *confirmed* the redefinition and opened the way for us to enter into this New Creation. Because of the enigma of the cross, we can now enter into intimacy with God unashamed, out of hiding, candid about our sin, forgiven, free, real, . . . and, oh yes, *holy*. But it is Jesus' *teachings of the kingdom of God* sandwiched in between Advent and Holy Week that redefine it all and gives to the church its unique character as *light* and *salt*.

Historically, the church seemed to have had this redefinition reasonably well grasped until the time of the emperor Constantine. Then, when "the empire" gave it acceptance, it succumbed fairly quickly to the seductions of wealth, status, and power. Such seduction caused it to revert to merely human concepts. And as the church forgot then, so it continues to forget and to operate by the former definitions. The idea of the kingdom of God has become simply a religious "gloss" on normal human definitions. The light reverts to darkness, the salt becomes saltless, and the true mission of the church is tragically compromised.

WHAT HAS ALL OF THIS TO DO WITH THE PRESBYTERIAN CHURCH?

How does all of the above relate to Jesus, to his heart, to his mission, to the Father's sovereign good purpose in Christ?

When one looks for the "why" of the Presbyterian Church's descent into chaos (from such a fruitful history), one slowly and yet increasingly awakens to the consciousness of Jesus *outside*, i.e., the "Laodacean pathology" institutionalized and accepted. Jesus is acknowledged in the creeds, sung about in the hymns, portrayed in the stained glass windows, . . . but reduced to a sacred relic. Jesus, reduced to a utilitarian name invoked in the liturgy, expected to bless, forgive, and take us to heaven, . . . but not to consume our hearts, not to transform our lives, not to demand our deepest loyalties. Jesus becomes marginalized and unreal to those called by his name. Jesus, at his own table of remembrance—body and blood—becomes a scheduled observance, the logistics of which become its focus, i.e., is it done "properly." Rather than a fervent coming to "Do this in remembrance of me" which brings us to our knees in joyous thanksgiving, it becomes something we do once a quarter as part of the church's schedule (which is better than not doing it at all, but leaves something of its intense relational and adoring essence wanting).

If the Body of Christ is to be the *Body of Christ*, somehow its life is going to have to be just such a sweet savor of Christ unto God. That is more than just a bunch of people "playing church" but rather a bunch of people who live by and for Christ, who are so consumed by his love and so formed by his word that he, himself, is the inescapable presence!

Am I a vain dreamer? "We beheld his glory, the glory as of the only begotten Son." So the church, as the glory of Christ, of God, of the new creation, . . . must be just that. And it is not very visible as such at this present moment. As Lesslie Newbigin puts it (in his discourse on the congregation as the hermeneutic of the gospel, i.e., that by which the gospel is interpreted to the world), "The reigning plausibility structure can only be effectively challenged by people who are fully integrated inhabitants of another."[6] And we are hardly that at the moment. Yet even that understanding *could be* simply an intellectual persuasion that did not consume the heart. Somehow both mind and heart must be persuaded and consumed.

The church is about Jesus Christ. And in the "Laodacean pathology," Christ gets overshadowed by a whole churchly ethos that is abundantly religious and well-intentioned but which does not flow out of the adoration of Jesus. It is a bit of an irony that even in the *Book of Order*, when recounting the Protestant watchwords (G–2.0400) of "grace alone, faith alone, Scripture alone," fails to include "Christ alone" with them. Rather it includes Jesus in a somewhat muted introduction to the watchwords. For Martin Luther, whose words these are, there was never any doubt that the door to it all was Christ alone.

Such forgetfulness may be one of the liabilities of second, third, or fourth generations of Christians, with our belief in infant baptism. We may have come to the point where the church is such a very familiar and comfortable part of our social fabric that we don't notice the "drifts." Such second and third genera-tions, not having been consciously delivered out of the darkness of unbelief, guilt, and the hopelessness of sin, are indifferent to (and not too emotional or thrilled about) *salvation*, and consequently about Jesus. The Spirit is quenched. Yet, at the same time, newer church expressions, built upon Christ-focused evangelism, are full of folk at the entry level of faith. They experience the joy of new life in Christ and are not only thrilled with Christ, but are eagerly trying to figure out how to reach everybody else, too.

What is embarrassing to our Presbyterian way of doing things is that such churches often have atrocious theological blank spots and aberrations. But they *are* enamored of, and thrilled by, Jesus. And so, Bibles in hand, they are bearing fruit. God chooses to use those foolish things whose hearts belong to him.[7] I am persuaded that the Presbyterian family has an indescribably great treasure of biblical and theological understanding which is rare (and much needed) in the larger family of God.[8] We have a belief that our minds are to be used in the service of God. But we have successfully kept our great treasure in a select enclave of ecclesiastical, clerical, and theological elites. Thus it has been so hidden from the public that it is essentially the "light under a bushel basket" which Jesus described in the Sermon on the Mount. But even more, we have somehow separated those theological riches from sheer devotion to Christ so that they have become blighted with a spiritual death that has kept them from bearing the fruit that God desires, either in transformed lives or transformed society.

We need to confess with broken hearts how lamentably much of our PC(USA) ecclesiastical "busy work" is carried on with little if any deference to Christ, other than a perfunctory prayer now and then. We must also remember that John Calvin not only offered God a finely-honed mind, but he offered it with a flaming heart in an open hand.

JESUS, JESUS' MISSION, AND THE KINGDOM OF GOD

The church is a useless institution and a vain enterprise unless it is formed out of adoration for God in Christ, according to the mission he gave to us. Unless the church (whether Presbyterian or any other) is a community focused in the worship of the glory of God in Christ; unless it is a community modeling New Creation in the midst of the old; unless it is a community of the Holy Spirit evidenced in lives of faith, hope, and love; unless it is a community consumed by a costly obedience to Christ's mission mandate which sees each individual, the whole of society, and all of creation as the objects of God's saving grace; and unless it sees the kingdom of God as God's sovereign, silent, and irresistible (and "upside-down") working in human history—the church will become one more merely human piece of religious entertainment, little more than a deceptive comfort zone for children of darkness who say "Lord, Lord" but have missed the whole point of Jesus' coming.

And so we turn now to that "particular stance within the history of God's people" which is our robust "*affirmation of the majesty, holiness, and providence of God who creates, sustains, rules, and redeems the world in the freedom of sovereign righteousness and love.*"[9]

4

Sovereignty:
An Absolute and
Not an Abstraction

SOVEREIGNTY. WHAT IS THAT ALL ABOUT? WE ONLY HAVE TO look at recent history for a stirring example. For seventy years the Soviet Union derided the Christian faith, espoused atheism, persecuted and outlawed the church, and declared that such nonsense was a "grandmother's religion." Guess what? When the Soviet empire collapsed and the masses were packed into Red Square to celebrate its demise, guess who was a prominent leader in the celebration? The patriarch of the Russian Orthodox Church. Great masses came to be baptized into the faith. And guess who were God's evangelists during those seventy years? The grandmothers. God's sovereignty and God's sense of humor. "I will build my church, and the gates of [death and] Hades will not overcome it" (Matt. 16:18).

What an incredibly exhilarating and crazy time to be alive in God's world. Everything is in flux. Change is dramatic if not diastrophic at every level. It is very much akin to the psalmist's " . . . though the earth give way and the mountains fall into the heart of the sea"(Ps. 46:2). Our high joy, wild hope, and exhilaration of faith come from our strong confidence in the Sovereign God who is our refuge and strength, our *constant* in a world of change. It is because of this rambunctious faith that we Presbyterian folk affirm "the majesty, holiness, and providence of God who creates, sustains, rules, and redeems the world in the freedom of sovereign righteousness and love."[1]

High in the Drakensburg Mountains of southern Africa there is now a narrow paved roadway that weaves among those stark and precipitous slopes. But at one time, it was a narrow horse path with not even enough room to lose nerve, turn around, and go back. On one side, walls go steeply up to the summits, and on the other, they drop precipitously off into the "you're-afraid-to-look" chasms. At one point, there is an especially tricky pass which was accurately nicknamed "Molimo Nthusa" by those early travelers. Molimo Nthusa translates as "God help us!"

The challenging and no-turning-back moment which stirs our blood and exhilarates us in our walk of faith and obedience within the Presbyterian Church is that we are at a cultural and ecclesiastical Molimo Nthusa (along with all of the other denominations). We cannot turn back. There is no way to turn one way or the other. All we can do is accept our own wonderful theological and biblical heritage, and know that it is going to be a time that will stretch everything in us and take us into realms of life's challenge that we have not experienced before. Everything moral and intellectual, cultural and emotional in us will be tested. Our confident hope for our future rests with the Sovereign God who is already out there, who is with us, and who purposes to make us expressions of his New Creation right in the midst of the chaos. It is this strong confidence that is our particular stance within the history of God's people.

The cultural and ecclesiastical chaos is more real than most (who are in current positions of church leadership) are willing to admit. The very concept of "denomination" is now living by virtue of artificial life-support systems. It is not that the ecclesiastical structures of the Presbyterian Church (which have been useful in the past) are *going* to change and pass out of existence, . . . they *already have*! Vital congregations indulge and endure their obligations to the governing bodies, but they actually conduct their lives and mission apart from them. They find support and accountability in numerous other relationships and ad hoc networks with those of similar belief and mission vision.

On the national and political scene, it is much the same. The consensus toward government that was essential in the minds of such framers of the constitution as James Madison is hardly present. Respect for government erodes amidst the secularity, cynicism, and confusion of the postmodern mind. The institutions of church and society find themselves in a very different cultural climate. Their usefulness is questioned, not trusted, and not at all guaranteed.

But this very chaos is our Molimo Nthusa where we move forward in the strong hope and mission vision that the present and future belong to God. In the midst of change, we are confident that God's New Creation, God's *redefined* ("upside-down") kingdom-dominion is the present, dynamic, and determinative reality. Church *structures* are nowhere guaranteed. God's *church*, on the other hand, is called out by God and will endure as his community of faith, as his missionary instrument, and by his decree. God will not be boxed in by hier-archical church structures, Presbyterian or Roman Catholic. God's dominion breaks forth in the most unlikely ways, apart from human plans and antici-pation, and in the most unexpected moments of the human sojourn.

So for us to confess *chaos* is not to say that God is absent, forgetful, or irrelevant. And certainly not that the whole thing is hopeless. Quite the opposite. There is a fascinating school of thought, which is currently affirming that *chaos* and *order* are not opposites but are in fact paradoxical—*ying* and *yang*—so that out of the chaos comes newness. This *chaos theory* is also of a mind that it is precisely those who embrace chaos as much as order who are the best prepared for the twenty-first century.[2] So our *Molimo Nthusa* is both to embrace and look forward to newness and to refounding our Reformed witness in the twenty-first century. Our chaos keeps us on tip-toe, knowing that it is the context of God's sovereign working.

There is a seemingly obvious truth that needs to be underscored at this point of our journey into *refounding* "this old Reformed house." That truth is that God's *sovereignty is not an abstraction*. Nor is it simply a locus in a text-book on systematic theology. God's sovereignty is not captive to or victim of anything in all creation (cf. Rom. 8:39). Though all of the forms of this PC(USA) may become history, its biblical and theological *raison d'être* (present in communities of those so convinced) will not pass away. It will, rather, become even more urgent and timely and thrilling.

SOVEREIGNTY IN ACTION

The New Testament opens with everything pointing toward a whole new reality which is breaking in upon the human and historical scene. Gabriel tells Mary that her child shall sit upon the throne of his father David and that his dominion will have no end (Luke 1:32–33). Mark reports Jesus coming upon the scene in his public ministry with the dramatic statement about the fulfillment of the expectation of the reign of Yahweh.[3] Mark puts it crisply, "After John was put in prison, Jesus went into Galilee, proclaiming the good news [i.e., *gospel*] of God. 'The time has come,' he said. 'The kingdom of God is near. Repent and believe the good news!'" (Mark 1:14–15).

Or in another paraphrase, "My dear people, you would be well-advised to wake up to reality and sort out your priorities, because there is upon your doorstep the presence of the ultimate, irresistible, altogether new, and radi-cally different intrusion of the sovereign God. Just call it the *kingdom of God*.

Oh, you're not going to see it. It is going to operate in ways you least expect. It will not come with any kind of spectacular and grandiose displays of pomp and power. Quite the opposite. But it *is* here. Don't mistake it. I am going to create a new kind of community made up of men and women who see it. You will see its evidences. And in the end, nothing else will matter. This is the reality of God's gracious design for his whole creation. It *will* happen. Your response? Choose what will be your ultimate loyalty. How do I know? Because my presence is the announcement. That's why I'm here." Matthew speaks of the beginning of Jesus' public ministry in much the same way. "From that time on Jesus began to preach, 'Repent, for the kingdom of heaven is near'" (Matt. 4:17).

What becomes obvious in the New Testament is that there are several descriptions of this sovereign intrusion of God into his own creation, all of which, if not synonymous, are so overlapping as to reflect the same reality. In the synoptic gospels, the term *kingdom of God* (or heaven) is the dominant one. John appears to speak to a different cultural setting and so uses *eternal life* to point to the same reality. So also, a case can be made that *salvation* and *righteousness* and *new creation* are all used to verbally paint the same picture of God's sovereignty at work in Christ. I would also like to make the case that the several different themes—sovereignty of God, mission of God, kingdom of God, gospel of God, and Spirit of God—are all inextricably interconnected pieces of the initiation, energizing, and irresistible working of God in human history. (Then we may want to factor in God's providence, mystery, left-handed surprises,[4] and serendipities, not to mention God's unpredictability and common grace[5]—and it does get a bit adrenaline-pumping, doesn't it?)

SOVEREIGNTY AND OUR REFORMED HOUSE

One speaks of the sovereignty of God and its implications only in an act of adoration of the God and Father of our Lord Jesus Christ. One stands or kneels in the presence of such glory much as Isaiah did, in a mixture of total broken-hearted contrition and overwhelming awe which brings us to cleansing and freedom with ecstatic shouts of joy, . . . and then to obedience. But one never deals with the attributes of God with bloodless scholastic curiosity; rather, only in the discipline of knowing God which leads on to worship and to new obedience in God's mission design for his world.

This focus on God's sovereignty has made those of us who are Presbyterians, who are Reformed Christians, the butt of a lot of grotesque caricatures in the secular media. We get hung with a lot of distortions about our "weird" beliefs, like predestination, and about our very strong convictions about the "party-pooping" will of God in the world, i.e., sin and all of that stuff. Our strong sense of biblically oriented faith is seen as some kind of a dull grey blight on human aspirations and upon our "fun." But this all can be attributed to the fact that humankind, in rebellion against God, has a false sense of human autonomy and of freedom that roils at any idea of a God who would infringe upon its vaunted self-sufficiency.

Anyone hearing this claim to "a particular stance within the history of God's people" might well ask, "So, don't all Christians believe this stuff?" Of course they do. "So, what do we have that does not belong to the whole Christian church?" The answer is *Nothing at all!* It is only that different traditions put their focus or their particular stance at different places in God's overall design. There are various gifts, and therein lies the beauty of a wonderful tapestry within the people of God. For instance, the Roman Catholic, Orthodox, and Anglican traditions keep before us the mystery of the church and the sacraments. It is a necessary reminder. Or, when our focus on divine sovereignty devolved into a sterile kind of determinism, it was God's gift of John Wesley that came forth to remind us that within the sovereign purpose of God was a mandate to preach repentance and to call men and women to faith. He obeyed, and the Wesleyan genius emerged as a vital missional movement with all kinds of beautiful dimensions.

Luther's focus on the grace of God in Christ, on scripture, and on justification by faith continues to be a rich and continual reminder to those who would forget. Menno Simmons' and the Anabaptists' wariness about the seductive nature of this present fallen world and emphasis on peacemaking are correctives to our endemic temptation to become too much a part of the world and to be seduced by its powers and conflicts. In this century, it is the awakening to the presence and power of the Holy Spirit within the church in the form of the Pentecostals that is a gift of God. Pentacostals were at first derided, scorned, and marginalized as a fringe sect. But then they began to infiltrate all of the major traditions. Pentacostalism began to mature and is now a needed and wholesome witness with the Body of Christ and a major missionary force. These and other witnesses, or gifts, all belong to the Body of Christ. They are all part of the tapestry and evidences of God's sovereign design. One can tune up the frequency on any of them and become divisive or cause some kind of theological aberration. But somehow in the mystery of the church and the working of the Creator Spirit, we all interact, correct, and nurture each other. We Reformed Christians are one witness within the whole, and at our best, we are a very necessary and wholesome one.

Yet in a collapsing culture without a sense of transcendence or absolutes, it is precisely this sense of the heart's true home and the sense of some transcendent purpose that lies deep within the spiritual hungering of my *twenty-something* friends. It is precisely this focus that is our Reformed gift to the larger "one holy catholic and apostolic church." When we pray "Your kingdom come and your will be done," we actually believe that God has a purpose for our lives and for this world in Christ. We are confident that God's name, will, and dominion are not at all abstractions. We really believe that the *kingdom of God* is irresistible and is presently at work in human history. We even believe that our praying is somehow part of that sovereign working. We believe that when Jesus came preaching the *kingdom of God,* he was not talking in some vague otherworldly (or devotional) language. What he was announcing without much subtlety was that through his presence in human history, God's New Creation was in fact being inaugurated right in the midst of the rebel dominion of darkness, and that it would move and flow silently and unobserved (Luke 17:20) until it was totally consummated at his own return.

Mind you, there is no *triumphalism* here. The very plain teachings of scripture go on to tell us that this kingdom will be accomplished at great cost, through much suffering, persecution, self-denial, and servanthood. The saints will often cry out, "How long, Oh Lord?" But God's purpose will prevail. The New Creation will be consummated. The day will surely come when the Lord God Almighty and the Lamb will become the focal point of all creation and the "temple" in a new heaven and a new earth. "The nations will walk by its light, and the kings of the earth will bring their splendor into it" (Rev. 21:24). What this means is that the sovereign purpose of God in Christ, the *kingdom of God,* is not one show among others. Rather, it is ultimately the *only show in town.*

THE MISSION OF GOD, THE SOVEREIGNTY OF GOD, AND THE GOSPEL OF GOD

At this point, some honest soul just might say, "Okay. Big deal. So what?"

I'll accept that question. Look again at the cultural context of our calling in the twenty-first century. The postmodern age, the quantum age culture that is moving into dominance, while fascinated by its own high technological and information age capacities, is at the same time a hauntingly empty culture without any overarching sense of purpose, transcendence, or absolutes. Robert Bellah noted that this young adult culture is marked by sullenness and hyperactivity. There is nothing to worship. Another called it disconnected and discontinuous, i.e., a culture of ambiguous individualism where nothing is connected and which has no story. Personal relationships are frequently carried out on the internet which, in fact, depersonalizes them, because they can be "clicked off" at will. "These . . . leave their home, become spiritually lost, are deprived of good work, seek refuge in illusory realms, fall prey to frivolous seductions, and forsake love's medicine for the anesthesia of therapy."[6]

Novelist Walker Percy describes the dilemma:

> How you can survive in the Cosmos about which you know more and more while knowing less and less about yourself, this despite ten thousand self-help books, one hundred thousand psychotherapists, and 100 million fundamentalist Christians. . . .

> or

> How it is possible for the man who designed Voyager 19, which arrived at Titania, a satellite of Uranus, three seconds off schedule and a hundred yards off course after a flight of six years, to be one of the most screwed-up creatures in California—or the Cosmos . . .[7]

"So what?" Look at the phenomenon of Kurt Cobain and the musical group Nirvana. Cobain and Nirvana emerged into high visibility in a very short time, apart from the normal route of high pressure promoters. He and the group somehow became the voice of despair for a whole segment of the younger generation. He himself was a product of divorced parents—a ping-pong-ball childhood—bounced from one parent or relative to another. When he and the group suddenly became rich and famous, his life was still without any meaning or hope. His music is like a loud primal scream of agony. The music is strident, loud, cacophonic, and accompanied often by wild and destructive performances by the musicians. What is amazing is the chord of response which it plucked in so many. Millions bought his music. He became their voice. When Cobain committed suicide with a shotgun, a wave of grief and greater despair descended upon his fans. How can we read that and not weep? Life without meaning, without hope, and without some answers to the "why" of it all is surely a nightmare, often anesthetized by empty hedonism, narcotics, endless listening to punk rock and grunge music, and by sullenness and hyperactivity.

Now the question: Where is the church, and what does it have to say?

Reality Check: God is the Good News

As strange as it may seem to ears jaded with too much politically correct secularity on one hand and too much religious junk food on the other, our

Reformed grasp of the glory and majesty of God-who-is-God; God who is Creator, Redeemer, Ruler, and Sustainer of the world; God of extravagant grace and infinite love; God of righteousness; God of justice and mercy; Lord of history; God who in Christ is the one by whom and for whom everything is made; God who is personal and has a name and wants to be known comes as fresh and living water to those dying of thirst. Such candid trust in such a God does in fact bespeak a distinctly *wholistic structure of meaning, purpose, and reality*. Such faith is not without foundations; it is not at all impersonal, purposeless, or fatalistic. It is good news that *the* God who desires (wills) that he be known, communed with, and adored is what everything in all of life and creation is about.

For the despairing and nihilistic and empty, our God is really, really good news. But note, this is the God made known in Jesus Christ and in scripture. We are not talking of some self-created subjective god or divine urge. It is the God and Father of our Lord Jesus Christ that is good news. Philosophically, this is our presuppositional view of reality (metaphysic). Life and the world and history have *meaning*. We define reality and meaning by the self-revealed God.

Truth Check: Good News! There is "Truth"

Every thinking person is either honest or dishonest about those *a priori* assumptions that are behind where all of his or her thinking begins. One assumes and confesses to some view of reality, or lack thereof, if one is intellectually honest. Persons who are otherwise very intelligent folk are often very dishonest about these assumptions and try to hide behind some claim of "intellectual objectivity." Atheism is as surely a faith position as is theism. It is a pure and simple religious stance, however much one attempts to deny it. It assumes that there is no god, and therefore begins its thinking from a metaphysic that can discount the divine hand in anything. The big "why" question can only be answered by the random *chance* of "natural" forces. So also the politically correct secular humanist, if he or she were honest, would realize that to assume that there is nothing beyond humankind's quest for fulfillment is, in itself, a faith position. (This is the folly behind so many of the American Civil Liberties Union's [ACLU] public protests.)

A person's thinking begins before the theory is proposed. There are presuppositions in all of our attempts to know and understand the meaning of our existence. They may be unprovable by scientific method, but they are very, very real. We Reformed Christians can be more honest than most. We can go public with our whole intellectual structure. We can candidly stand in "missionary confrontation with the world" (cf. Newbigin), and do it with good will. We can lay it all on the table for public scrutiny. And we can challenge others to do the same. We can say that we know because God has spoken. God has not left us in darkness. God the Creator has willed that we know him, that we begin our thinking with him, and that we listen carefully as he speaks through the prophets and apostles and most especially through Jesus Christ. Facts, for us, are not brute facts floating out there, disconnected from anything. Withal the mystery, legitimate doubt, and areas of the unknown, the Reformed Christian is witness to a view of knowledge (epistemology) that begins with the presupposition of "the God who speaks." That is also really good news to the despairing who are searching, tired of dead-ended human answers to their deep cry for their hearts' true home. It is the very witness that the postmodern, post-Christian, quantum culture needs desperately to hear. It is also a word that my *twenty-something* friends long to hear.

This is also where we Reformed Christians come down on the nature of scriptures. These sixty-six books are a miracle in themselves. We come to them with the belief that they are somehow the vessel of God's revelation to humankind, the Spirit-energized record of God's interaction with real people in real history. We know that scriptures contain all kinds of literary genre and are fraught with mystery and problems of interpretation. But all that being so, scriptures are somehow also alive and their *plain sense* is there for all to engage. Because of this, we Reformed Christians look to scriptures as the vehicle of God communicating to us—even communicating to us across the centuries what we know about Jesus, the revelation of God in flesh and blood.

Truth check—*epistemology*. There is a word from the Lord.

Behavior Check: Good News! We Know How to Live

Autonomous humans have always resisted any limitations on their behavior. Look all the way back to the biblical story of Eve and Adam (Gen. 3) who bought into the metaphysical and epistemological proposition the idea that God had no right to tell them that one fruit was off limits. History is a record of the desperate quest for freedom which has only led to deeper bondage and confusion. The postmodern culture is devoid of any absolutes. This may sound wonderfully liberating, but in fact it has become horribly enslaving and destructive. Our Reformed witness, which derives from the above themes of reality and truth, is that we humans are not only God created, but created in the image of God. We understand that we become most truly human, most blessed, and most free as we live in harmony with God as he has revealed himself and his will through Jesus Christ and the holy scriptures. This being so, our true *shalom*, our true freedom, is found by living in willing harmony with God's own being and will. This places limitations on our aberrant quest for independence and autonomy. The very revelation of God, namely that God has made us for himself to be expressions of his own *glory* (i.e. the expression of his own creative being and will), sets us free to really be *free*.

It also means that there are moral and ethical absolutes for us, which determine our behavioral responses (ethics). God has spoken this freeing word very clearly. From the beginning, God has given us principles by which to live in true and worshipping harmony with himself, in loving relationships with each other, and in responsible stewardship towards all of God's good creation. The Torah in the Old Testament and the Sermon on the Mount (the New Torah) in the New Testament spell out for us those principles by which we are to love God with all of our hearts and our neighbors as ourselves. These moral and ethical absolutes, these *kingdom principles of behavior* are what serve as the *inertial guidance system* in us in all of our relationships whether in economics, human sexuality, politics, environmental stewardship, or societal obligations. They are critical especially in times of such cultural chaos as ours. And note, they also define the church and the *Reformed household* as a New Creation community. This community is, by virtue of its calling, an *ethical community*.

The malignant darkness of *this age* ever seeks to erode, to qualify, or to deny these ethical implications of the sovereign God. Our *Christian-theistic metaphysic, epistemology,* and *ethic* make us "different" even "alien" to a world and society of men and women whose assumptions ignore or deny the reality of God, truth, or absolutes. When the poet said, "It has been lonely in the world since God died," he was lamenting how terribly desolate is our human *existenz* without a sense that the God of justice and caring also inhabits it all with us. It is just such a desolate and empty outlook that is bringing so many of our human community to such despair, sullenness, and hyperactivity. It is our strong conviction that such a self-revealing God enables us to offer these same people our witness of "caring and celebration,"[8] i.e., communities of worship and of true love, hope, and faith, not to mention communities of intellectual honesty and toughness. The twenty-first century will cry for this witness even more poignantly.

WELTANSCHAUUNG: WHOLISTIC GOOD NEWS

Weltanschauung is a fun word. Don't you like it? It is a good word to pull on your friends and see if it impresses them. It is one you learn while reading intimidating volumes of philosophy or theology. But it is really a very good and descriptive word. It is a word that describes an intellectual and faith stance which is so all embracing that it sees everything, all of life and reality and history, as having a coherence in an overall purpose. Our Reformed stance has been just such a witness to the church and the world. It is a wholistic view of what God has come to accomplish in Christ. Nothing gets left outside of this good news. We Reformed Christians are very insistent and self-conscious about holding to a *Christian-theistic weltanschauung* with its attendant view of reality, knowledge, and behavior. We do not allow any dimension of God's creation to exist apart from our understanding of God's sovereign good purpose in Christ. Our *weltanschauung* sets us free to explore, question, investigate, and probe every area of creation. It even gives us freedom to doubt, to leave unresolved some mysteries, to be agnostic about some things. But it gives us framework and context for life. When the Christian church begins to forget this, it begins to lapse into minimalistic, provincial, partial, or truncated conceptions of the gospel of God. It has forgotten and does forget.

That intellectual movement called the Enlightenment, with its exalted sense of the autonomy of human rationality, consigned religion to the private or inner and personal opinion of the practitioner. Religion was not to be allowed in the public square, nor was it allowed credibility in the academy. The church, tragically and far too much, bought in to this line. Little by little, it became improper to allow one's "religious prejudice" to become too visible in life outside of the church (and often inside the church). This erosion ate away at the foundations of the Christian church's *weltanschauung* for the several centuries which we call the Modern Era. The whole "faith versus reason," and the "science versus religion" controversies arose out of this forgetfulness. The secular *weltanschauung* more and more prevailed, until we find ourselves now in the bewildering postmodern culture in which nothing coheres and where there is no framework.

As the vaunted claims of modernism continue to collapse around us with the onset of the quantum age, it is fascinating that the fields of science and philosophy are where Christians are emerging into prominence. Christian men and women of science are asking for the presuppositions and the *weltanschauungs* to be laid on the table and for colleagues to come forth with answers to the scientifically unanswered question of "why" or "what for." It is here that our particular (Reformed) stance is so timely. Its wholistic understanding of what God is doing in all of his creation and in history gives the context to evaluate all kinds of things.

The environment is a case in point. As the environmental crisis looms larger and larger in the public mind, the church has awakened to its own denial of its God-given stewardship. Christians have been captive to partial and truncated understandings of their own Christian message. This is not to mention captivity to the rapacious greed of the market economy that has despoiled so much of the environment. The church has forgotten that it has a stewardship mandate toward all of the environment. Reformed environmentalists have been at the forefront of coming to grips with, and awakening the larger church to, its responsibility here as an implication of its wholistic gospel, which grows out of its Christian *weltanschauung*.

SIN: MISSING THE POINT

It will be helpful to stop here and see if we can clarify slightly the idea of *sin*. In biblical writings, sin can either be some individual behavioral aberration or it can be the designation for the whole darkened *aeon*. But sin is not primarily some catalog of things that violate rules. It is just plain missing the point of God and God's purpose. It is completely screwing up because we haven't read the instructions. When the apostle says in Romans 3:23, "All have sinned and fall short of the glory of God," he is talking about life that is attempted in isolation from God's created design. I have a tough time understanding this word processor that I'm using as I write this. So I have a helpful book entitled *P.C.s for Dummies*. When I read and figure out what the design and purpose is, it works. When I try to invent my own solutions, I usually get into big trouble and spend a lot of money calling in some computer whiz to untangle me.

All of God's creation is constituted so that it operates with God's *shalom* when it is lived in harmony with his creative design and purpose. When we leave God out of the equation, or attempt to redesign God to meet our own convenience, it begins to be destructive and runs amok. What we're learning in the vast church establishment in the West is that it also becomes dysfunctional when we truncate the gospel to make it congenial to the dominant social order or the plausibility structures of the world around us. When we conveniently leave out some God-given principle or set aside some God-given ethical guideline, a virus begins to corrupt the whole.

History and the history of human thought and philosophy are a fascinating record of the human attempt to make sense out of life, to explain what we are doing here, and to fabricate some political, intellectual, or economic structure that will bring us back to Eden. Messianic proposals abound. But when the whole point of it all is missed, it self-destructs. When God is trivialized in human experience, the darkness envelopes it. And that is where we are at the start of the twenty-first century. This is not neutral territory. This is rebel territory and it is *into this rebel territory*—variously called the kingdom of darkness, the kingdom of Satan, this present evil world, or the aeon of this cosmos—that

Jesus came, inaugurating his own rightful sovereignty. Only, he doesn't play by the rules of the darkness.

It is not as though Jesus arrived in a vacuum to announce his new creation. It was rather in the face of very real rulers, principalities, powers, and kingdoms, whether corporate, ideological, religious, political, tribal, . . . or whatever. Biblically, there is a pretender after sovereignty who is called Satan and who inhabits and is called the ruler of this world. The context, the ethos, the malignant and alive reality of the darkness is subsumed under such descriptions as "the evil one," "the dominion of Satan," etc. And it is into just such structures of commonly accepted darkness that Jesus and God's sovereignty intrudes with a silent, irresistible, and totally different and new reality called the kingdom of God.

I am belaboring this *redefinition of dominion* because the church has a hard time getting it. We keep reverting to type and employing old definitions. When scriptures assert that "he must reign until he has put all his enemies under his feet" (1 Cor. 15:25), it is to be understood that he will do it in his own upside-down kingdom where "the foolishness of God is wiser than man's wisdom, and the weakness of God is stronger than man's strength" (1 Cor. 1:25). We need to remember that Jesus triumphed over principalities, that he was manifest to destroy the works of the devil, by being "defeated" or executed on a cross. Isn't that amazing? Yet it is so far from the triumphal thinking and denominational preoccupation with prestige and institutional prosperity that we live with.

Contemporary voices of concern and alarm about the erosion of culture tend to focus on one or another dimension of this domain of darkness such as pornography, materialism, dismal politics, environmental pollution, corporate greed, indifference to social needs, or ethnic hostility. Yet all are part and parcel of this same fabric of darkness and these various dimensions linked symbiotically with each other. There is systemic darkness of which the individual darkness is but a part. But note, our Reformed heritage is very cognizant of this malignant darkness and its expressions. The falleness of creation is also presuppositional with us. And it is in the context of this darkness that God's sovereignty is not an abstraction, as contradictory as that may sound to those who are still blind and deaf to the kingdom of God. It is a kingdom of grace (which includes common grace, i.e., God's goodness to that which is still part of the darkness and those who don't believe to do good things).

God is working out his own purpose. God is not stymied, chagrined, or "faked-off." But when any church takes on a life and agenda of its own, when it reverts to the wisdom, power, and prestige of this age, it is bypassed and becomes part of the darkness, until such time as it repents. But when any church remains faithful to Jesus and the principles of his dominion—though it may suffer all kinds of deprivations, toil, and conflict—it becomes an instrument of God's sovereignty. The kingdom of God, which is the new creation of God and where his upside-down sovereignty invades the scene of darkness, is also full of humor or irony and hilarious episodes. Just consider the humor of the last chapter of Acts, for instance, in which we find Paul in Rome, in the shadow of the Roman forum, proclaiming the kingdom of God. In that place where the salute was to affirm that "Caesar is Lord," the Christian underclass (primarily) said, in essence, "Sorry about that, but Jesus is Lord." In the midst of the Pax Romana, a somewhat nondescript peasant from the periphery of the empire is heralded as the Prince of Peace.

That is sovereignty. It is not an abstraction. At this very moment in history, after seeking to evangelize the subcontinent of India in all kinds of ways over the last two centuries, there is a huge turning to Christ among the lowest of the low in India, the "untouchables." These persons, who have never even had names given to them, have been found or apprehended by the sovereign Lord and have had their eyes opened to his love. Tens of thousands are turning to faith in Christ, and at baptism, they are given a real name for the first time. They are important to God. Upside-down? Nothing less. It is not where we would have planned an awakening, but God's sovereignty has that special way of exalting the helpless.

What's going on in the world? What is before us in the twenty-first century? Well, get a good grip on your Reformed *weltanschauung* and fasten your seat belt because God loves this world—loves it sovereignly—and will use those persons and those churches which are in synch with his kingdom principles. God will continue to insert himself into human affairs with his different kind of rules and his hidden, quiet, and mysterious interruptions, . . . and he will often use those who are humanly least likely to accomplish this new creation. Look for God's providences and left-handed surprises. The realm of the Spirit is expressive of that sovereignty. The Spirit opens eyes, creates new life, changes hearts, and rearranges priorities.

We Reformed Christians in this old Presbyterian house have tried our best to tame this lion. We have a process of democratically electing leaders. We have standing committees to deal with issues. We have *Roberts Rules of Order* to assure that it is all done properly. We have safeguarded our venerable doctrines with ordination standards, seminaries, and master of divinity degrees (we thought). And in all of this we have succeeded in effectively quenching the Spirit under the rubric of "decency and order." What God is looking for are those good and faithful servants who, out of lives of worship, give themselves to joyous and holy obedience to be God's servant-disciples. He is looking for those who are living out the principles of the New Creation and so are becoming light in the darkness and salt in the corruption.

So it is time to confess our folly and return to our roots in which we adore the God who is majestic and holy, and who creates, sustains, rules, and redeems the world in the freedom of sovereign righteousness and love. And it is time to reintroduce this God into the public discourse in faithful witness to the Sovereign One whom this rebellious world so desperately does not want to meet, . . . and yet so desperately needs.

FROM PROLEGOMENA TO PRAXIS

These first four chapters have been foundational. They are our *faith assumptions*. But they have implications which reach deeply into every dimension of our daily lives. In your *Book of Order*, you will find several specific areas of the praxis of our Reformed faith (G–2.0500) which we will use for our general framework, and I will also add a couple of others. But please don't disconnect these first four chapters and especially chapter 2. Someone made the telling statement that if our lives are not integrated with Christ's Great Commission, then our lives are irrelevant to history. These practical dimensions, then, are expressions of our *new creation lives* which are essential to our faith and proclamation as we express the love of God for the world.

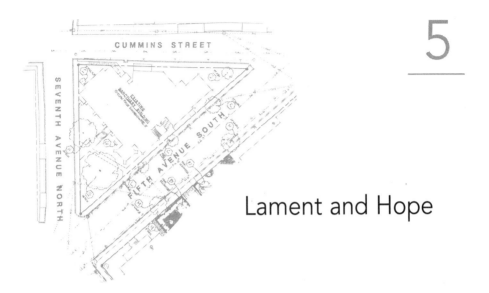

Lament and Hope

BEFORE WE CONTINUE WITH THE BLUEPRINT, WE'VE GOT TO LAY a body to rest. Let me tell you a story to illustrate what I mean. Roger Vieth has been a friend for many years. He has had a distinguished career as a neurosurgeon. I baptized Roger when he was still in medical school and met with him for prayer every Saturday morning during those training years. When he was chief resident in neurosurgery, the department in which he trained was probably the best in the world and was very demanding. I remember one Saturday morning in particular when he came to our breakfast and prayer time and was very disturbed. The night before there had been an auto accident, and a star basketball player from a neighboring university had received a severe trauma to the head. He had been brought to the emergency room in hopes that he could be saved. Roger's description went something like this. "Bobby, there he lay, one of the most beautiful physical specimens I have ever seen. Every part of his body was perfect. Except there was nothing we could do. The head injury was so severe that he was clinically dead. We could keep him alive on artificial support systems, but he was dead. It was sad. So beautiful, so athletically gifted, . . . and so dead. I felt so helpless."

I have some of the same emotions writing this. The history of the Presbyterian Church has been so remarkable and has produced such blessing; yet more recent decades have brought decline, trauma after trauma, along with cultural shifts that make such denominations no longer a factor in the thinking of most, . . . and the time comes to make the decision to confess our denial, remove the artificial life-support systems, and acknowledge that the

PC(USA) as a functioning structure of Reformed faith and witness is no longer viable, i.e., dead. As an evangelized and evangelizing instrument of that "particular stance within the history of God's people" [G–2.0500 (a)], . . . forget it.

LOST CONSENSUS

What brought the Presbyterian Church into being and caused it to be able to cohere and operate as a vital functioning structure of Reformed faith and witness was a three-fold consensus, outlined as follows,

1. The first was a consensus on the missionary *raison d'être* for the church's existence as given by Christ. This is obvious in the *Book of Order* which begins with the classic "Great Ends of the Church" in chapter 1, then continues with the theological content of that missional focus in chapter 2, and comes back to the missionary consensus in chapter 3. This has produced wonderful episodes of missionary obedience in these several centuries of Presbyterian history. But as forgetfulness set in, along with equivocation on the uniqueness of Christ and Nicene Christology, the missionary consensus became problematical. This, along with the Enlightenment optimism, concerns the human potential and the eventual legacy of Protestant Liberalism. The latter is offended by the idea of lost-ness and divine judgment, not to mention the universality of faith and the validity of other world religions, rendering the missiological dimension of the church severely qualified and evangelism an embarrassment. So there is no longer a missionary (or missiological) consensus.

2. Then there was a theological consensus that we all mutually held to a particular focus on the gospel (translate gospel as *thrilling announcement*) of God, which, for lack of a better term, we call *Reformed*. This is our heritage from a sixteenth century genius by the name of John Calvin, who saw the gospel of God and the glory of God in a wholistic framework. Calvin looked through the lenses of scripture and saw everything, . . . *everything* as the arena of the glory of God in Christ. Not just the church. Not just the individual. Everything. This focus was unique among the reformers. He taught us to see God's hand at work in places we would least expect it. Question: "Why did God make you and all things?" Answer: "God made me and all things for his own glory." That question from the child's catechism reflects the common faith of the Reformed family. Reformed Christians were evangelistic about the fact that the sovereign

God was irresistibly working out his good purpose in a new creation that would ultimately consummate in a new heaven and a new earth wherein dwells righteousness.

But generations of forgetfulness, carelessness, preoccupation with success and survival, and this larger "founding myth" (i.e., the initial beliefs, values, and mission) have faded from the corporate consciousness of the rank and file of Presbyterian folk. There is no discernible strong conviction of Reformed consensus left on the whole.

3. The third point of consensus was on a form for the missional and Reformed community created by the first two. It needed a structure of mutual encouragement, responsibility, and accountability through which to give form to the common life of our Reformed life and witness in the world. From scripture there emerged the concept of a church from which the godliest persons, i.e., the most mature in their knowledge and experi-ence of the gospel, most gifted in teaching and disciplemaking, and most exemplary in life and relationships, would be set apart by the congregation to oversee the life of the community. These were the *Presbyters*, the elders. There was to be a provenness of life within community of faith so that there would be what we call a *Spirit-filled* leadership. These elders would be accountable to one another, and together they would be responsible to lead the community in faithfulness to the gospel in life, belief, and mission.

Again, this was a point of consensus. Then various Reformed commu-nities of faith entered into covenant with each other for mutual support, accountability, and mission. These became the regional presbyteries and the larger General Assembly. But several centuries eroded this into a vast structure of polity that took on a life of its own, with an ever expanding constitution that has guaranteed neither faithfulness in faith nor mission.

At this moment, we have consensus in none of the three.[1] All of the former attempts to nurture such a Reformed witness in church and in worship, by way of catechisms, colleges, seminaries, and ordination standards, have long since been lost as fecund sources of such. Catechisms fell into disuse, not to mention the disdain of sophisticated *avant-garde* Christian educators. Colleges and seminaries became enamored of academic acceptability and captive to intellectual *zeitgeists*, and ceased to be motherlodes of Reformed thinking, creativity, and vitality. Reformed voices in these institutions are now marginal. And one wonders what theological education and ordination standards even guarantee, . . . other than academic ability.[2] And meetings of governing bodies are either a bore or an embarrassment more often than not.

In Company With Isaiah

We are not the first of God's people to come to such a confusing moment, when a rich heritage lies desolate before us. Think of Isaiah. For over forty years, he faithfully looked at Judah and Jerusalem in their disobedience and forgetfulness of the covenant and proclaimed that disaster loomed inevitably on the threshold. In its days of glory, Jerusalem had been described by the psalmist; "It is beautiful in its loftiness, the joy of the whole earth . . . is Mount Zion, the city of the Great King" (Ps. 48:2). Generations later, Isaiah looked upon the same scene and lamented that "The city of meaninglessness lies desolate; . . . all rejoicing has reached its eventide" (Isa. 24:10–11)[3].

But Isaiah's lament was suffused with his message of hope and future, which transcends the immediate moment of disaster. God had not died. God's purpose had not changed. Even the covenant with Israel stood. It was not God who was unfaithful, nor was he forsaking his promises. The coming demise of Judah and Jerusalem would be times of chastening and cleansing and would be the next step in God's unfolding purpose in grace. But it would take a major calamity to bring this holy nation to its senses, to confession, and to a return to covenant faithfulness. It would never be the same. Yet it is in the context of Isaiah's writings that we have our most eloquent prophecies of the Messiah to come (which Judah and Jerusalem could not even comprehend at this point in the eighth century B.C.E.).

So it is with us at this moment. As we stand at the threshold of the twenty-first century, it is a somewhat ominous (or exciting) moment for the PC(USA). At this moment, all biblical and confessional integrity is on the line. Historical revisionists, theological and biblical deconstructionists, and hermeneutical sleight-of-hand artists have done their work with such effectiveness that the foundations are undermined everywhere. The *epistemic* faultline becomes more obvious, creating two worlds of discourse that cannot be bridged by mere polity.

Still, . . . that's not the whole story. Yes, particular Christian forms can and do die. Denominations die (or merge into nothingness). Congregations die. Mission organizations die. But God doesn't die. God has an almost mischievous way of operating in the most unexpected and left-handed ways. Just about the time we have our eyes fixed with despair upon the human hopelessness of some scene, . . . count on it. God will break forth in some totally creative and totally serendipitous expression of his good purpose in Christ. And if one continues to look with human eyes on the human hopelessness, one might just miss it all.

Seeds of Hope

Just as a human body is conceived by the gift of life as husband and wife come together in the act of procreation, so when their bodies die, the life they have conceived also has the gift of life and passes it on to another generation. This wonderful mystery of life is also related to our present moment. Though we look now on the death of our Presbyterian parent, that seed of life (created by the Spirit of God) that brought this church into being has not died, but has been reproduced in many children in strange ways. As a functioning structure of Reformed faith and witness, the Presbyterian Church may now be dysfunctional and on life-support systems (clinically dead), . . . but this doesn't mean that the Reformed life that conceived it and its heritage has died, nor has God's intent that his glory be the focus of his people.

So while the Presbyterian Church is more and more like a comatose and elderly parent needing constant and expensive care, which will not forestall its demise, it is those fruits of its health in children and grandchildren that are our hope for the twenty-first century. The *Reformed household* we are seeking to put into blueprint form will be built upon those episodes of evangelized and Reformed life that can relate to the *postmodern* and *post-denominational* culture of this century. It is the emerging generation that has the capacity of transformational life that glorifies Father, Son, and Holy Spirit.

I thought of this a few weeks ago while listening to John Perkins address a sizable Presbyterian congregation. John is a remarkable Christian community developer who laughingly refers to himself as a "third-grade dropout," which he is. As a black native of Mississippi who was converted to Christ as an adult, he is also a wonderful trophy of God's grace in the way he thinks. Scottish theologian Ronald Wallace once exclaimed with excitement (after hearing John speak), "He thinks just like Calvin!" John sees all of life wholistically and sees the implications of the gospel of Christ beginning with the individual and the church, and then moving out into society with a sense of God's initiative and energizing; he does in fact display the genius of John Calvin. What kept running through my mind was how embarrassing it was to have a third-grade dropout energizing a Presbyterian congregation with the very message that is their own heritage. God uses the foolish things of the world to confound the wise. I thought, Where are all of the thousands of M. Div. recipients who should be teachers and practitioners of this very kind of Reformed thinking? I had never heard the sovereignty of God so convincingly set forth, nor the purpose of the sovereign God in bringing light into

America's urban darkness so compellingly stated.

There is a humorous bit of turf guarding that goes on in many institutions that can't accept anything "N.I.H." (Not Invented Here). John Perkins wasn't invented by the Presbyterian Church. The sovereign God, who is the focus of Reformed understanding of the gospel, is not confined to its structure. So, when it forgets its own message, God has a way of bringing in from the margins a prophet to remind us. It is also fun to look at all the things that we didn't "invent" that are remarkable for their life and fruitfulness. In the field of missions, the effects of missionary obedience and faithfulness crop up all over the world. Many of the parachurch missionary movements are founded by, or led by, Presbyterian folk. It is interesting to contemplate that some of the most vigorous Reformed thinkers now hold prestigious faculty positions in universities that are not in any way related to the Presbyterian and Reformed family, such as Fuller Theological Seminary, Notre Dame, or Yale. And this is not to mention the host of remarkable Reformed scholars and pastors in other denominations. God is full of surprises, but given Calvin's robust confidence in God's sovereign good purpose, I don't think Calvin would be surprised.

Congregations and pastors, without any help from the denominational structure, produce fruit, engage in mission, and struggle with how the sovereign God intends for members to function as agents of the Reign of God in daily life. Pastors and teachers who want to refine their Reformed thinking must network, trade bibliographies, and meet together to be sure the heritage from John Calvin makes it into the twenty-first century.

Now, strange as it may seem, nearly all of this is somewhere stated in our constitutional documents. But when the consensus evaporates in forgetfulness, even the constitutional documents don't really have much effect. But these existing materials of Reformed life and awareness are the very materials out of which will come the post-denominational *Reformed household* of the twenty-first century. The very trauma of the demise of the PC(USA) will waken this sleeping giant, or genius, to the blessing of the whole of God's church. I say that quite deliberately. I don't see the *Reformed household* of the twenty-first century so much as a denomination but as something like a versatile "Reformed Order" within the "one holy catholic and apostolic church." It was the late John Mackay who prognosticated that the future of the church might well belong to "a matured Pentecostalism, or a reformed Catholicism, or a combination of the two!" Prophetic?

Whatever the future holds, it will not look anything like that which we have experienced in the past century.

BETWEEN PARADIGMS: CONFUSION

What, in all reality, are dead are the vast denominational structures of all the mainline denominations, of which the Presbyterian Church is but one. It is not that they will disappear overnight. Hardly. But they will become increasingly marginalized, archaic, ineffective, and ignored. They will continue to downsize. At the same time, most of the visible denominational furniture is still in place. There are, at this moment, still something like eleven thousand Presbyterian congregations, and one can charitably assume that one-half or two-thirds of them are somewhat viable communities of Christian faith and evangelical life. There are still 2.5 million "Presbyterians" inhabiting these congregations. Some of these still possess strong Reformed convictions. Some are more generic evangelicals without Reformed self-consciousness. Some are only what has been humorously designated as "denominational franchises." Many, also, are the result of the pious agnosticism which is the fruit of the Enlightenment and of Protestant Liberalism, and they have little of a biblical faith component left. Many are basically independent and congregational, despite the denominational label. In the post-denominational era, some will choose to go a different route. This is all to say that we are looking at a period of ecclesiastical confusion (chaos) that could last up to a decade or more.

Our question is how to faithfully respond to this reality. As the paradigm of the *denominational* era is replaced by the radically new paradigm of the *post-denominational* era, the denominational disenchantment and detachment will force local sessions to ask the questions we have been dealing with here; Why do we identify with this denomination? What is our connectedness and consensus? What on earth does all of this have to do with our constitutional consensus? Or more, what does it have to do with Jesus' mandate and mission for his church? Does it enhance our mission? Does it have life? Is there some better way to cooperate in mission and accountability? How do we relate to the larger holy catholic Church?[4] There will unquestionably be some confusion, some wandering, some church closings, some realignments, and an increasing number of *ad hoc* networks.

BUT NOW, . . . HOPE!

There are in human history those fascinating transitional moments. I tend to think that we are living through one of them. Biblical commentators make an interesting point in their expositions of such an epistle as Romans. They note that Paul will record all the history of human darkness. But when he exclaims, "But now, . . ."⁵ or "But God, . . ." you are alerted that the saving initiative of the sovereign God is going to break forth in some fascinating episode of New Creation. So we are at that "But now, . . ." moment. Missionary Horace Fenton says that the sure-fire formula for missionary failure is to look at the impossibility of the task, look at the meagerness of your human resources, and then, . . . *leave God out!*

The tragic mistake that anyone would make in looking at our future is to leave God out of the equation. Anyone with Reformed eyes will be looking at the cultural decay and the denominational demise with the excited assurance that God never forsakes God's own sovereign purpose to create all things new. Expect something quite *unexpected* and more than a little thrilling.

WHAT WILL IT LOOK LIKE?

I am willing to risk a prophecy, namely, that out of this present chaos will come a smaller, chastened *Reformed household*. It will be renewed and energized by the Spirit of God. It will be articulate and self-conscious of its "particular [Reformed] stance." It will move into the twenty-first century evangelized and evangelizing with its transformational faith in the sovereign God's immutable intention. This intention is to bring light into the darkness, to rejoice the earth. Missional creativity so conceived in prayer will motivate it to glorify God in all of God's creation as, irresistibly, all things are made new. This will involve both the transformational living and thinking, as well as the evangelizing conversation, of God's people as they are demonstrably New Creation folk in daily life. Such hope in Christ is the foolishness of our preaching. It is all so humanly unlikely, if not impossible, . . . *except for the impossible possibility of God's "But now, . . ."* Our calling, then, is not to rush off in human energy and seek to reinvent some denomination. It is, rather, to go back to our theology, and beyond that, to go back to our *adoration*, to go back to God and God's calling in Christ.

BACK TO "THIS OLD HOUSE" AND GENERATION X

Yes, don't leave God out. Don't overlook God's "*But now.*" In this very unlikely period of our Presbyterian sojourn into the *post-denominational* era, God is birthing a new generation which is not like any we have seen in many generations. It is a generation disconnected from its parents' world and a generation in discontinuity with history in general. These X'ers are fed up with the ambiguous individualism fostered by the modern society and embraced by their parents. They live without any integrating transcendence to give meaning to their sullen lives. The sterility of rationalism that disenchanted the world has made them open to the possibility of an enchanted world indwelt irrationally by spirits and angels and demons, . . . and God. Lack of intimacy in relationships has created a pathological loneliness.

Now back to our "This Old House" metaphor of chapter 1. When we finally strip away all of the unwanted structural distractions which have been added by way of conformity to culture and by forgetfulness, and we get back to the inner integrity; . . . when we get back to the essence of this Reformed structure, what is going to be apparent is that this very Reformed essence (so eclipsed in recent generations) is going to be the key evangelizing point of contact with Generation X. When the archaic forms give way to *Reformed essence*, a new form will certainly emerge.

Why do I say this? Because as we look with missional eyes at my *twenty-something* friends in Generation X, we are looking at people who are spiritually hungry. They will be unable to express this hungering in theological or even familiar traditional terms, but they are hungry all the same. What they long for is hope, meaning, and transcendence. They don't want discourses, sermons, or word trips. They want reality and the experience of something they have never known.

Richard Mouw has a wonderful illustration that makes my point. He tells of being at a concert of the Rolling Stones along with eighty thousand screaming fans. Mick Jagger was racing back and forth across the platform screaming his song "I Can't Get No Satisfaction," and the fans joined in. Over and over again, "I Can't Get No Satisfaction." Into Rich Mouw's mind came in counterpoint the old Psalter version of Psalm 42; "As pants the hart for cooling streams, . . . so longs my soul, O God, for Thee . . . ." "I don't get no satisfaction!" "As pants the hart for cooling streams, so longs my heart for Thee." *Exactly!* The Spirit of God creates in the human heart a longing for its true home, and that's our message. God is working in Generation X, creating the longing and the climate for Jesus and New Creation.

And as a missional church which believes that the sovereign God is working to bring all things under the gracious reign of Christ, we need to listen with ears attuned to what the Spirit of God is doing to make ready the hearts of this new generation. Then we must be active in crafting a form for this *Reformed household* to demonstrate New Creation and hope to these X'ers, who really aren't interested in our denominational pride or church institutions that reflect the meaninglessness they are rejecting.

What will the communities of this *Reformed household* look like? Let me venture some descriptions. First, they will be demonstrations of New Creation that will be beyond rational explanation. They will stand in awe of that *weltanschauung* (discussed in the last chapter) that results from their utter confidence in God's sovereign working in Christ and in human history. They will accept the mystery and wonder of scriptures, with all of the diversity and literary forms contained in these documents, as somehow God's instrument of making known to us who he is, who we are, and what's going on in this world. This will be energized by that transcendent meaning so beautifully expressed in the hymn:

> This is my Father's world: Oh, let me ne'er forget
> That though the wrong seems oft so strong,
> God is the Ruler yet.
> This is my Father's world: The battle is not done;
> Jesus who died shall be satisfied,
> And earth and heaven be one.
>
> —Maltbie D. Babcock

With minds fully engaged and hearts responsive to God's word in scriptures, the dominant idols of our culture will be exposed as the darkness that they are. *Holiness* will no longer be a "no-no" description, but will characterize a people consciously seeking to live and think *in synch* with the very God who has rescued them from the darkness. They will become part of this household, knowing that God intends that their lives be conformed to the likeness of Christ.

Gatherings for worship will be suffused by and motivated with the wonder at the majesty and honor and glory of God that will motivate them to lives of sheer thanksgiving and adoration. This will express itself in prayer, praise, and wholehearted, expressive worship in the Spirit, with all that such means in silences, song, rehearsing of scripture, and profound involvement in that which the eye has not seen, nor the ear heard. And the fruit of such worship will be lives of joyous obedience in God's mission.

Communities will form around such an understanding of the *Reformed household*, and other communities already in existence will be *refounded* by such. Some communities from other traditions without a clear self-understanding, looking for their true home, will become part of this household. The door will be open both to and from other traditions within the holy catholic church. Because the missionary, redemptive, and transformational heart of the sovereign God will beat strongly in his children, these communities will seek out the places of darkness and destruction, and intentionally relocate there to bring the Light. But more than that.

With such a sense of God's sovereign good purpose in Christ and in redemption, these communities will look at and study the intractable social pathologies of their localities, and with a rambunctious, obedient, and imaginative faith, they will become the incarnation of God in the midst of these realities. They will in fact be the salt and light that God intends. This is to say that the *Reformed households* will be self-consciously New Creation communities. They will have a missional identity so that any and all who identify with them will accept that missional sense. Streams of living water will flow from committed communities of worshipping, thoughtful, obedient, and creative disciples.

Ancient hymns will throb with rediscovered life and meaning. New hymns will be written to express the joy, wonder, and knowledge of God in Christ. Pianos and organs will be joined by electronic keyboards, drums, flutes, brass, and strings. Worship will be a release of mind and emotions in response to such a God, such holiness, and such unimaginable love and grace. Along with heartfelt and expressive praise will be a hungering and thirsting for the voice of the Good Shepherd which will take engagement with scriptures to new levels.

One more thing. In the *post-denominational* era, and as this *Reformed household* emerges, we will come more and more to rediscover and appreciate two things from the past. First, along with its own focus on the "majesty, holiness, providence of the sovereign God who creates, sustains, rules, and redeems the world in the freedom of sovereign righteousness and love,"[6] . . . the Reformed household will also rediscover and be blessed by the other great traditions of the larger church. It will be blessed by the Anglican and Catholic sense of mystery of the presence of Christ in church and sacrament; by Luther's jealous zeal concerning the centrality and sufficiency of Christ and his atoning work on the cross; by the Anabaptists' sense of the seductive darkness of this world and their identity as an alternative and peacemaking people; by the Wesleyan reminder that the predestining God also commands the preaching of repentance and faith to call women and men into new life in Christ (it doesn't just happen); by the Orthodox understanding of the gospel as incarnational; and by the Pentecostal emphasis on the life-giving Spirit. These, at the least, are essential.

The other rediscovery will be that the history of God's people doesn't begin with this generation, but that many others in many locales and times have struggled with their pilgrimage in tragic and difficult encounters with the darkness. This will mean that as the Christians of the twenty-first century struggle with the postmodern realities of neo-paganism and cultural decay, they will look with new appreciation at church history and at the great creeds and confessions of the church, and those historic milestones will come alive with new relevance and encouragement.

Am I a vain dreamer? I certainly am, and unapologetically so. Ken Medema has so poignantly stated the need for dreams in his song "Is There a Place for Dreaming":

> Is there a place for dreaming
> in the corners of your mind?
> In a world where dreams are broken,
> and dreamers hard to find
> do you dream and weep sometimes
> about the way that things should be?
> Come dreaming with me,
> dreaming with me,
> admission is free. . . .
> [Now that I'm grown] I find that life
> with no dream is a desert that . . .
> I can not bear.
> So if it's all right, I'd like to open
> my mind and see if my dreams are
> still there.[7]

Lament and hope: that's where we are. We live with both. We are in transition from one familiar and fruitful episode from the past, acknowledging that it is now no longer viable. But from that rich heritage, we understand that our God is God, Sovereign God, Redeemer God, who gives to his people a joyous future and a hope. And so we have.

Our purpose from this point is to go on with our blueprint for the twenty-first century. Every blueprint has what are referred to as "specs," i.e., the specifications for the building. This *Reformed household* will be made up of God's people, but as a Reformed people, there will be certain characteristics that will continue to give us our special form and witness. For these "specs," I shall rely on three primary sources: (1) from our own constitutional documents, I will rely on chapters 1, 2, and 3 of the *Book of Order*; (2) I will use my mentor John Leith, especially his *Introduction to the Reformed Tradition*; and (3) for a sense of the requirements of the future, I will use Lesslie Newbigin, *The Gospel in a Pluralist Society*.

The *Reformed household* holds thrilling missionary potential for fruitfulness in just such an "impossible possibility" challenge as we are now confronting in the twenty-first century. We will begin with those who are to be the agents of the New Creation and what that involves.

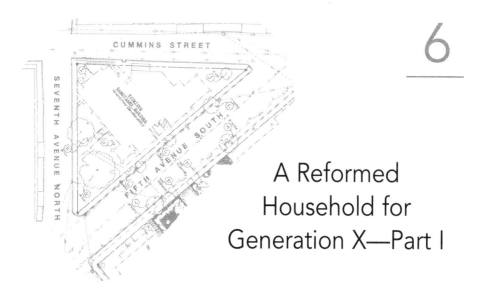

6

A Reformed Household for Generation X—Part I

UP TO THIS POINT, I HAVE BEEN DESCRIBING SOME OF THE foundational materials that I see in any twenty-first century expression of that which we have known as the Presbyterian Church with its Reformed tradition. We're closing in, now, on our *Blueprint 21*, and a conversation posed the initial question for me.

SO, WHO NEEDS IT?

I had been sharing all of this (the stuff in the first five chapters) with a small group of my *twenty-something, Generation X* friends. As I got to this point in my enthusiasm for a Reformed household, I was stopped mid-sentence by a vivacious X'er. She was really trying to be polite, but I could tell it was a struggle. "Hold it!" she broke in, "You are obviously convinced that all of this stuff you're talking about is really important. It even has some interesting dimensions, like it's good stuff. But I've got a confession to make. First of all, a big 'So What?' And secondly, I don't have a clue what you're talking about. The Presbyterian Church is a non-factor in my Christian life, though I'm a member of it. And whatever *Reformed* is all about, it doesn't exactly boot-up my system! So, bottom line: Like, who needs it?"

I really loved her response. It's sort of like ice water in your face (plus a megacup of Starbucks Coffee) to wake you up to the reality of a generation programmed differently. It also says in bold print that . . . *if* there is going to be a *Reformed household* (by whatever name, and whatever form it might emerge) for Generation X and for the twenty-first century, *then*, . . . it is *not*, repeat *not* going to have too many similarities to that Presbyterian Church whose demise we are lamenting here. It is going to have to be much more attuned to the cultural realities of a strange new cultural neighborhood, to a radically different and alien culture. It is also going to have to comprehend much more self-consciously and, of necessity, internalize that which is the energy and the *culture-creating essence* of the Reformed heritage. It is going to have to disenculturate itself from the sixteenth through twentieth century expressions of that heritage. And, face it, most of this has been buried in forgetfulness in the church we have known and experienced.

And we do actually need to answer the question Who needs it? If it is a fascinating piece of history whose day has come and gone, we can lay it to rest. But let's review where we have been, as part of seeing where we go next. In the first chapter of this *Blueprint*, I likened our project to that of the "This Old House" program of public television. The point I made was that there certainly is something of enormous value hidden in this decrepit old Presbyterian house. That "something" is the perspective on the good news of God which we have given the designation of the "Reformed" tradition.[1] It is not the exclusive property of the Presbyterian or Reformed Churches, but it has been our particular focus and witness within the family of God. It is, as we must always remember, only one of the rich traditions that are part of the tapestry of the "one holy catholic and apostolic church" of our creeds.

We have projected a *Reformed household* which would be the expression of this focus into whatever the *postmodern* and *post-denominational* context of the twenty-first century looks like. In the ensuing chapters, we looked at the *missional* priority of the church, then at the priority of *focus on Christ*, and finally on the *sovereignty of God* and the implications of that (which is the focus of Reformed thinking). Finally, in chapter 5, I confessed my lament over the demise of the Presbyterian Church we knew in the twentieth century and my hope for the twenty-first.

LIKE, WHO CARES?

Next question, Who cares? And who do I propose will be the agents of such a project of refounding this *Reformed household*? Surprise! I am looking at what may humanly appear to be the most unlikely source of candidates, namely these very *twenty-something, Generation X, Baby Buster* friends. Does that surprise you? Sound incredible? But hold on. There is good reason to predict this. It is going to be their very spiritual hunger, brutal honesty, and entrepreneurial skills that are going to see and expedite our blueprint for the twenty-first century. And I believe they will do it with a contextual sensitivity and an evangelical intensity (not to mention a biblical integrity) sufficient to create a contagious mission movement of remarkable proportions. Many of these future pathfinders are even now in our colleges and seminaries with spiritual and intellectual juices flowing.

And why do I predict this? Simple. Look at history. It is always the younger Christians who rise to impossible challenges and to reckless obedience. They are still free in their spirits to enter uncharted territory, take on the risks, and be adventuresome. We are at the first stages of a cultural disruption such as we have not had since the end of the middle ages. It was the youthful reformers of the sixteenth century who led the way for the church to be delivered out of its past and into a new cultural setting. There had been reforming movements along the way that had been snuffed by the hegemony of the Roman Church. The Renaissance had been used to open the windows to winds of fresh thinking and biblical studies.

Onto the scene came several adventuresome and spiritually restless young men to give momentum and form to this movement which we now call the Reformation. Martin Luther was the "old man" of the reformers but was only in his early thirties when he challenged the dominant order (or the darkness). Calvin was about eighteen when he emerged as a spokesman for reform while a student in a French university. Others such as Melanchthon and Zwingli were also young, bright, and willing to challenge the system.

It is almost axiomatic that the older that folk become, the more they are captive to their security and resistant to taking risks. They tend to cling to present patterns and have difficulty imagining anything different. The young reformers saw darkness in the church and called it just that—darkness. I have the same anticipation for Generation X. The older Booster-Geezer (pre-World War II) generation is over the hill and not looking for too much "boat rocking." They identify with the Presbyterian Church that they have known all of their lives. The Boomer generation people are too culturally captive and ambivalent to be the creative agents of such refounding (though they often see the need for it). So I put my money on Generation X. I think it is X'ers who are going to be the ones who *care*.

Let me, now, make a partial response to my X'er challenger who didn't know what in the world I was talking about. Let's take a shot at what it might well look like. Let's pick a date and begin to see if we can put our imagination into some tangible *blueprint* form. Such futurizing is risky at the least, if not foolish. But perhaps we can at least spell out some of the structural basics.

THE STRANGE NEW NEIGHBORHOOD OF THE YEAR 2020

Let's pick the year, like A.D. 2020 (or C.E.). That gives us about twenty years for our cultural diastrophism and ecclesiastical chaos to begin to sink in and become glaringly obvious even to the most obtuse. The missionary confrontation between the Christian faith and the darkening neo-pagan culture will be the daily reality of the church by then. The church will probably be even more suspect by the dominant social order by then. All of the polite respectability which it enjoyed in the modern era will be history. The Constantinian agreement (co-option) between church and culture will no longer pertain. Christians will be "resident aliens" in spades. By then the Booster Generation, who dominated the twentieth century, will either be dead or in care facilities. The Boomers will be flailing about in retirement, eating more low-fat yogurt, still trying to figure it all out, and coping unrealistically with their age.

But by then the *twenty-somethings* (Generation X) will be the *forty-somethings* and at center stage. And they will be looking at all of this strange neighborhood and at the church with a whole different set of cultural eyes.[2] And, please note, it will be the radical contrast which will provide the church with its long overdue self-realization that it is, in fact, a *missionary* community, the *alternative* community demonstrating God's new creation in the midst of the old. Here are some pieces of the strange neighborhood in which it, and Generation X, will be incarnate.

Life Without Center or Connectedness

The culture of 2020 and of Generation X is a culture that has no center and no connections with the past or its traditions and institutions. Neither will it have much hope for the future. X'ers have been described as a generation that is disposable, disconnected, discontinuous, and decentered. Even relationships are illusive. Making acquaintances on the internet is hardly a context for true intimacy. The marital and familial erosion in the Boomer culture means that their children have hardly known true community in the sense of responsible family life or healthy intimacy. Virtual reality will have blurred the boundary between the real and the fictional, between reality and unreality.

Life Without Absolutes or Authority

Imagine life without absolutes, without any concept of universal truth, with no true religion, and no unifying consensus on reality, and you have a picture of where we are in 2020. The culture of 2020 will be one in which all values are local constructs, community determined. It is a culture in which there are no absolutes in morals, no overarching norms, in understanding of reality. There is certainly no consensus in anything called truth. As a matter of fact, the idea of cultural consensus, of any "universal," will be dismissed out of hand. The idea of truth, a true religion, or attempts to establish one, will be met with a "get real" (or "who cares") derision. Even the use of language will be malleable. Rationality will not be all that important, so contradictory (irrational) styles within art or architecture, and disjunctures in religion, clothing, morals, and lifestyles will be easily accepted—just so long as it "works for me!"[3]

Life Beyond Old Loyalties

There are reasons to assert that loyalties to political parties, patriotism and nationalism, and companies and corporations will be a thing of the past. As a matter of fact, there will be cynicism directed toward all of these. These loyalties so dear to the modern era will dissipate with the growing sense of both global community and pragmatic localism. Internationalism will displace older allegiances to nationalism and flag (though governmental structures will continue to exist to provide some necessary services). Candidates for office will not be chosen because they are of one party or another, but because of how they relate to immediate and pragmatic concerns of the electorate. The large corporations will have long ago forsaken their right to any corporate loyalty by dehumanizing the work force and allowing economic considerations (greed), rather than humane and environmental concerns, determine policies. Newer, smaller, flexible, and more specialized companies will emerge—which will also be disposable when their function is completed. This will also apply to the former denominational institutions (such as the Presbyterian Church) and their traditions. But new kinds of loyalties will be emerging to fill the voids.

Life in a More Austere Economy

The realities of limitations in natural resources, human need, and a sense of global responsibility, along with competition from other peoples, forebode a much more chastened and spartan economy over the long haul. This does not mean that it will be unhealthy, nor will there be much that provides creature comforts and the continued role of technology. It does mean that the myth of unlimited growth that prevailed at the end of the twentieth century will have proven to be just that—a myth. Patterns that created the growing disparity between rich and poor will be tempered. The consumer economy will be replaced with a much more modest and demanding lifestyle for our X'er friends as the twenty-first century progresses. This will necessitate drastic revisions in the materialism that energized the former economic optimism with its myths. The church will have to come to terms with this also. The church's vast real estate holdings along with expensive institutional and programmatic expressions, so long marketed as "the church," will be sobered[4] and refined into essentials and integrity.

Life in a Thoroughly Cosmopolitan Neighborhood

The mass migrations will have reduced Euro-Americans to a minority in North America. As Asians, Hispanics, Indians, and Africans take their places of increasing prominence in the economic and political community, this new minority status of the Western traditions will become traumatic for occidentals. With the arriving ethnic majorities will come not only cultural baggage but the religions of the world (other than the Hebrew-Christian monopoly of earlier prominence). These religions will compete for loyalty among Generation X'ers with their acceptance of pluralism, localism, and their vast spiritual hungerings (and lack of discernment as to where they look). The vigor of Presbyterian Christians from places like Korea and Africa will increasingly be the formative influences.[5] Emerging forms of Christian community and worship from ethnic and generational sub-cultures will compete with and challenge older traditions. Likewise, the socio-economic and educational scene will also become much more cosmopolitan.

Life in the Information Age

In 2020 there will be little cloistered knowledge and few secrets. By the end of the twentieth century, there were already whole curricula and whole encyclopedias, as well as virtual sex and accessible pornography on the internet and on computer programs. So by 2020, institutions of higher learning and libraries, as well as all the vulgar expressions of pagan society will also be accessible into every home and apartment. Schools, colleges, seminaries (as well as Christian nurture programs) will be drastically reconfigured (if not totally irrelevant). At the same time, the more corroding expressions of the pagan darkness will also have access to every child and adult. It is a "Pandora's box" of possibilities for good and ill. Academic degrees will have become of only marginal importance. And the international community will be in communication in ways hardly conceivable to the previous era.

Life With Unfulfilled Spiritual Hungerings

God has a wonderful habit of seeing where his children dwell in darkness and then bringing them the light in non-traditional ways and from unexpected directions. This very postmodern culture, without roots, without intimacy, without hope, without universals, without connectedness, and without much sense of identity and place in this bewildering world, . . . will have also created a vast and desperate spiritual hungering that screams in the night and increasingly resists the frustrations of the pagan darkness. Count on it. A major awakening is in the offing for the X'ers! The heart's true home, that *longing for transcendence*, is still the Creator-God, however much that God may be disdained and marginalized (even denied) as the Alpha and Omega of all things by postmoderns. That very longing will be one of the doors that the Missionary God will use to reach the lost of the twenty-first century. It is also the key to the movement that will refound the Reformed household.

THE REDISCOVERY OF DIVINE SOVEREIGNTY

The transcendent God. Nothing flies in the face of postmodernism so much as any concept of One God, who makes exclusive claim to being Creator of all—the beginning and the ending of all things. There is nothing more ridiculous to or rejected by postmoderns than the idea of a God who is unique, Lord of all, sovereign, God of gods, and Light of lights, i.e., *the* God and Father of our Lord Jesus Christ and *the* God revealed in the Bible. That there is such a God who also makes himself known, who reveals his heart, mind, and will to his creation, is incomprehensible to postmodern thought patterns. It is this very "foolishness," however, that will be the keystone and joyous message of that wonderfully subversive community called *the church*. In a world of pluralism and locally constructed "truth," such a thing will be easily dismissed with a lofty scorn as unworthy of discussion.

Even so, it is just such a transcendent One, who knows and cares, that Generation X'ers long for, even inarticulately.

It will be within this alien and minority community of the followers of Jesus, with their subversive mission, that such a God will be demonstrated in alternative living. This God will be the *presupposition* which defines all of life. This sovereign Creator and Redeemer God will be celebrated in joyful adoration and in a renewed fascination. God's involvement in human lives and history, and in his remarkable incarnation in Jesus, will call forth lives that will be salt and light to the decay of the culture. The heart's true home will call forth a whole *new creation* of men and women who bear his likeness and love in the midst of the darkness.

In chapter 4 we tossed up the concept of a Christian-theistic *weltanschauung* (that fun German word) to express the wholistic world view that is so much a part of the Reformed stance. In a postmodern culture that rejects any world views, this concept will be totally out of synch with all of the plausibility structures of the year 2020. But it will also speak to the longing for meaning and transcendence among the X'ers. For one thing, such a wholistic view does not isolate faith and spirituality from all of the realities of God's creation. It is for this reason that Reformed Christians[6] have looked at their *redemptive-subversive-Reign of God* role in the institutions and structures of society. The missionary context discussed in chapter 2 will provoke creative and redemptive solutions, rather than dismay by the awakened and evangelized X'ers.

The presupposition of the sovereign and transcendent God who has wonderfully made himself known and has become immanent in Jesus and in human history, is the church's joyous faith. It sets people free to take a deep breath and rejoice that there is such a God. God is both personal and presently at work by his own sovereign Spirit in the church and the world. The God in whom we believe is the God who is involved with us in our lives and history. He is God of the nations, God of history, God of the past and of the future. He is the God who is merciful and extravagant in grace and love. The God in whom we believe also will not be boxed in by human design or church institutions. Nor is he boxed out by any cultural antagonisms. In God's faithfulness to his own eternal dominion, he keeps breaking forth in thrilling surprises of his power and grace.

Such a Christian-theistic *weltanschauung* has marvelous implications. It will be rediscovered by X'ers in the midst of the growing darkness that denies such transcendence. It will give the Reformed household a wholesome context in which to embrace paradox, wonder, mystery, doubt, and unknowns. It is not intimidated by the intellectual fluidity of the quantum age, nor the contradictions of postmodernism, structuralism, and the adventure of living in the midst of such. Reformed Christians have an inertial guidance system which sets them free, i.e. God is both free and freeing. God's sovereign good purpose in history and in Jesus Christ defines life's purpose. Intellectual curiosity incites research, and scientific discovery will only expand their horizons of God's creative design.

Reformed Christians are also incorrigible optimists, even in the midst of the most distressing and intractable darkness and struggle. This is because they see the challenges and complex problems of this present age (this sinful and broken world) as arenas where God rejoices to exhibit his sovereign grace. Such a faith also accepts and energizes the impossible mission and evangelistic mandate of Jesus, i.e., that of making disciples of the nations. Such faith knows that beyond all human agencies is the reality of God's providence with the surprises (serendipities) of God's irresistible love and power. Such faith walks with joy and anticipation into every new cultural setting. Such a way of living and thinking can never be captive to any culture or time, but is, in fact, transforming in every new cultural setting, politically, economically, socially, vocationally, personally, and familially. The culture of postmodernism will be only one more challenge to the irresistible grace and recreative power of God in the community of such faith. But, again, note that the result of such will not necessarily look like any patterns we have known in the past.

Reformed Christians possess a wholistic vision of the missionary mandate of God—"As the Father has sent me, even so do I send you."

REDISCOVERY OF ROOTS: THE ONE HOLY CATHOLIC AND APOSTOLIC CHURCH

As the post-denominational culture of 2020 erases so much of the connectedness of the church and its history, there will emerge simultaneously in Generation X the quest to know what the church is and where it came from. The excessive individualism of the culture in which the X'ers were formed will create an opposite and equal sense that there must be some larger Christian community that has roots back into the past. There will be a rediscovery that the church is rich in history, in its missionary expressions in the generations, and in the various cultures of the world during these past two millennia. Not only so, but there will emerge a sense that the church in the first several centuries experienced a culture with the same intellectual and spiritual stresses that we are experiencing in this post-Christian era.

From the historic creeds will come the discovery that the church defined itself as "one holy catholic and apostolic."[7] So long quoted mindlessly, this will blaze into new life and meaning. That the church is the community and demonstration of the dominion (reign) of God in the midst of the perennial attempts to destroy it will give the church in 2020 a sense of identity and hope in the daily encounter with the pagan darkness.

The Church as One

The church as the community of God's New Creation will have reasserted the unity that Christ prayed for. The alien context of the dominion of darkness in 2020 will make the former sectarian and internecine rivalries among the traditions incompatible with the common mission of the people of God. More than that, the church of Generation X will look with new eyes at its *oneness* in the midst of a vast and fascinating diversity of gifts and expressions. Eastern, western, old, new, Orthodox, Catholic, Protestant, Pentecostal, crazy missionary movements, and new forms and ministries which don't even necessarily identify with any of the above tradition, will all be embraced with new appreciation.

This sense of oneness will include the educated and uneducated, the poor and wealthy from Hispanic, Korean, African, and Indian cultures and sub-cultures who are called through Jesus Christ and by the Holy Spirit into a unity of faith and ministry under Christ's authority. This unity, or oneness, has the aroma of redemptive and filial love written all over it. The Reformed household of 2020 will appreciate its symbiotic relations with all of these other households. It will appreciate also that it has a ministry both from and to the rest of this wondrously diverse church of Jesus Christ. This oneness also flies in the face of the resistance of such a unity within postmodern thinking.

The Church as Holy

From the beginning, God called out a people to be expressions of his will and character, i.e. holy. The church, as the demonstration of God's new creation in Christ, is also called to such holiness (i.e., life *in synch* with God). Holiness really got lost in the later days of the modern era. It became a description that was to be avoided as Christians sought to be relevant to the cultural and moral *zeitgeists* of a increasingly pagan society. It was so diluted in the quest for inclusiveness and pluralism as to be meaningless. That God has always called his people to be *holy* will be rediscovered by Generation X in their 2020 incarnation. This alternative community with its alternative lifestyle that demonstrates the transforming life and power of the Holy Spirit will be a critical factor in the church's witness to the world. The life and ethics of this holy people will be defined out of their intimacy with their holy God. It will be nurtured in the community of the New Creation and in its worship.

The Church as Catholic

As the X'ers of 2020 rediscover their roots, the awareness of the true catholicity of the church will fascinate them more and more. Catholicity has to do with the awesome *everywhere-ness* and *always-ness* of the church Jesus is building. It reminds us that our own small experience of this community needs to be informed by the expressions of it that are so diverse and rich. The rambunctious obedience of missionary movements, the profound adoration and worship in classic liturgies, the small communities of eager Christians who minister to their crumbling communities, the companies of artists who convey the faith in creative forms of landscaping, painting, music, and dance—all are embraced with this concept. Catholicity reminds us that some have the gift of keen minds with which they serve God, and some have the gift of tender hearts that tune in to human lostness. The Irish monastics (c. sixth and seventh centuries) obeyed in devotion that was unbelievably costly, and that still astounds us. Koreans have a prayer life that has been a strong rebuke to the prayerlessness of the church in the west. The pilgrim church of the year 2020 will rediscover that major struggles over the nature and content of the mission of God go all the way back to the beginning. We are not alone. We are one part of something that is eternal and awesome in its expressions. Catholicity will be rediscovered with mutual joy and surprise by the church of 2020.

The Church as Apostolic

In its quest for life, integrity, and fruitfulness in 2020, the church of Generation X will rediscover that the church has always looked to apostolic writings for the understanding of its mission and its message. The writings of those immediate apostles of Jesus Christ define *apostolocity*. This quest for faithfulness to the apostolic teachings is the ongoing task of the church and is what energized our Reformed household in its beginnings in the sixteenth century.

Early on, the church took a well-meaning but ineffective turn by making "apostolic succession" a formal and institutional matter of the succession of the "laying on of hands." This practice did not at all guarantee the church's faithfulness to the missionary task, nor its proclamation of apostolic teachings. The church of the modern era has attempted the same thing by trusting in graduate academic training to guarantee faithfulness in mission and teaching. This also was well intended but has not succeeded in any consistent way. Still the Spirit of God is the dynamic agent in creating the church and continues to call forth those surprising persons and influences and movements that do call the church again and again to its apostolic focus.

It is here that our own Reformed tradition has been uniquely focused. In the sixteenth century, Calvin saw the need for a thoughtful understanding of biblical teachings, which would equip the laity for their daily work as the people of New Creation. As Calvin's heirs in this tradition, we have continually (but inconsistently and fallibly) struggled to link disciplined minds and flaming hearts in an engagement with (a) the understanding of the mission of God as set forth in Christ and the scriptures; (b) the exegesis of the culture in which we have been called to know that into which we have been called; and (c) to understand how we effectively, faithfully, and compassionately engage in this calling in our day to day lives as children of light. The superficiality and subjectivism (and often mindlessness) inherited by the church from the late twentieth century will create a desperate hungering to reclaim this apostolicity. This hungering will significantly give shape to the Reformed household's own mission of providing informed, thoughtful, and faithful understanding and living of these apostolic teachings for the larger church in 2020.

In a very real sense, as my X'er friends are reminding me, most of these things we have discussed are common roots that belong to all of the Christian church. They are, moreover, major structural pieces that will be rediscovered within "this Old House" and will become major parts of our *Blueprint 21*. So on to the specifically Reformed pieces.

A Reformed Household for Generation X—Part II

REDISCOVERY OF THE REFORMED (AND REFORMING) MATERIALS

Again, at this point in my sharing of this material, in all of my zeal, another of my impetuous X'er colleagues brought me back to earth. "Hey! We got into this to see if there was anything in this relic which we call the Presbyterian Church worth our efforts. Everything you've predicted has only suggested that somewhere in the mix is a Reformed (and nebulous) 'something.' But all you've said thus far could be said of almost any Christian expression in 2020. We're waiting!"

Right. But the integrity of the Reformed expression of Christian understanding is not disconnected from the rest of the one holy catholic and apostolic church. Still, there are some particular reforming principles that have helped and that will always be instrumental in the church's faithfulness in God's mission in the world. So let me go to the *Book of Order*,[1] as well as some other Reformed sources, in order to reclaim these valuable structural pieces.

RECLAIMING THE MISSIONAL FOCUS

At this point, I am going to have to ask my readers an indulgence. This is not an excursion, but it is essential to our task. I want to adjust your lenses. I want to give you a major reforming principle that most often gets missed (even by Calvin). Take note: *Mission is the mother of theology.*[2] Or in our case, *Missiology is the mother of theology.* To understand the church and the place of its theological reflections properly, we have to recognize first of all that the apostles, the New Testament writers, perceived from Christ that the people "called out" (i.e., the church) were to be a *missional* community. "As the Father has sent me, so I am sending you" (John 20:21) looms large in their thinking. When you see this, everything takes on a very sharp missional focus (in contrast to a custodial and institutional focus).

The advent of God in the coming of Jesus was heralded with this statement:

> He will be great and will be called the Son of the Most High. The Lord God will give him the throne of his father David, and he will reign over the house of Jacob forever; his kingdom will never end (Luke 1:32–33).

This begins the account that is increasingly awesome and gains momentum as we read the documents. For in adulthood Jesus comes to inaugurate his public ministry. Here is Mark's account:

> After John was put in prison, Jesus went into Galilee, proclaiming the good news of God. "The [appropriate or expected] time has come," he said. "The kingdom of God is near. Repent and believe the good news!" (Mark 1:14–15).

A telling moment came in this brief public ministry when he called his own intimates to a decision about what this whole thing was about.

> "But what about you?" he asked. "Who do you say I am?" Simon Peter answered, "You are the Christ, the Son of the living God" (Matt. 16:15–16).

Jesus accepted this as the heart, or the valid interpretation, of his presence, life, and mission among them.[3] Then he announced that upon this reality he would build his *church*. He uses a word (εκκλησια) which refers to an assembly called for a specific purpose. His assembly will be called out to be the people of this Messianic reality and mission. Note that *he* will build it. This is a people to be called by God into a new reality. That new reality involved being identified with him in what he was doing in the world. Mission—the Reign of God. Jesus' prayer recorded in John 17 essentially offers up to the Father his own faithfulness in this self-defined mission. His prayer then passes the same mission on to this infant community. He gives it the mission along with his own intercessions not only for them, but for those who will believe through their lives and words. The prayer is dynamic and throbs with expectation.

The evangelistic call of God to follow Christ is a call to be altogether converted out of one dominion (of darkness or Satan) and into another dominion (of God or light).[4] It is a call to be self-consciously engaged in the purpose of God, which is to exalt the name of Jesus in all of creation until every knee bows and every tongue confesses that Jesus is Lord. To be a follower of Christ is, to be sure, a call into the family of God with both the blessings and the demands. It is a call into all the blessings of forgiveness, adoption, justification, and a New Creation life empowered by the Holy Spirit. But never miss the point that it is also a call to obedience and into an alternative life of the New Creation. It is a call into God's mission so that those called will be the *walking, talking demonstrations* of that reality. The New Testament and the community of believers is quite incomprehensible apart from this sense of the mission of the children of light in and to the cultural darkness and its unbelief. The first several generations saw miraculous missionary penetration to the boundaries of civilization.

A COUPLE OF WRONG TURNS ALONG THE WAY

Someone observed that the Risen Lord gave this infant church the utterly impossible and ridiculous task of making disciples of all the nations. Image it. Here he was, an executed criminal no less, handing this tiny group such a universal task. Amazingly, though, he also gave them the enabling power to do it by the Holy Spirit. So long as they obeyed the missionary task and did what they had been called to do, they actually did move in awesome power against overwhelming odds. The church grew in quantum numbers. "But," this observer noted, "when the church dug in to conserve its gains, like the manna in the wilderness, it 'bred worms and stank.'" Graphic description, but not bad.

After the church's amazing life and growth, and obedience against the powers of darkness and the Roman Empire, something happened. In the fourth century, the emperor Constantine turned to the Christians to help him with a rapidly crumbling empire. He made an agreement to give them acceptable status and prestige, and they in turn would pray for the empire. This *Constantinianization* of the church may have looked absolutely wonderful after three centuries of pain. But it essentially marks a point of sadness in which the church was co-opted by its environment and diverted from its alternative consciousness as God's aliens and exiles. Rather, it became the established religious institution of the dominant social order (chaplain to the empire). This was the first wrong turn.

Then it took a second wrong turn. From an alternative community and a missional people, the church began to grow more and more into a *custodial* institution with priesthood (clergy), rites, and stability.[5] The intent was to assure order. The effect of this, however, was a more and more passive laity who became oblivious to their own missionary calling and character. To be a Christian was to be part of the established religion, to belong to the church, and to be subservient to the clergy. Empire and church became somewhat indistinguishable.

The point is that this drastically changed the focus of the church from a dynamic and missional community—alive, empowered, and gifted by the Holy Spirit—to a custodial religious institution, hierarchically organized with an active class of clergy (or "religious") who were the "professional Christians." Then the rest were the sheep who followed the clergy in a somewhat passive dependent fashion. From being aliens and exiles, they became the empire's religious support group. And basically these were two wrong turns. In the centuries that followed, there were surprising and continual breakouts, as anointed men and women saw (rediscovered) the missional calling and obeyed. But such breakouts were aberrations from the custodial norm.

When *mission* is obscured in the hearts and minds of the people of God, and when the church as a missionary people is in eclipse, even the church's biblical and theological study becomes an end in itself. It can even become incestuous. The Protestant Reformation rightly sought to understand what were the apostolic teachings. But too often they did it in abstraction from an understanding of apostolic mission.[6] Theology became an intellectual exercise and a tool with which to debate other Christians (all of which may have its proper role), but the church remained mostly indifferent to God's great compassion for those still "outside."[7]

So, we in the twenty-first century have inherited a church that (1) has been "*Constantinianized*," and (2) is *custodial*. The *clergy-class* was deemed necessary as the custodian of the institution. At the same time, these clergy were not necessarily set apart because of their gifts proven within the local Christian community, but because they were trained in the larger church's rites and theology. They were ordained because they could perform the sermonic and liturgical rites, along with the custodial role among the near passive laity. Ordination became the institutional prerogative and rite to give legitimacy to these in the eyes of the people and approbation by the ecclesiastical establishment. Meanwhile such qualities as maturity of discipleship, capacity in disciple making, loving ministry within the company of believers, fruitfulness in Christian obedience, skill in scripture, and maturity in Christ were (tragically) not always necessary to that ordination.

The laity, likewise, devolved into something of a support system for the clergy. They essentially became *second-stringers* in the church's life (even though many of them demonstrated far more maturity in Christian life and understanding than clergy). And what seldom makes it into popular church histories are all of the unexpected breakouts or the missional "end runs," in which God called and anointed unlikely men and women. There are wonderful episodes of those who do, in fact, have the life and power of the Spirit, and the Spirit sends them to do the work of mission. It is these who reclaim the church's missional role and remind the church of God's serious intention to declare his glory among the nations. To be sure, this is something of a sweeping caricature. But it is a very legitimate one.

Now as we approach 2020, the Constantinian agreement is rapidly dissipating in the context of a more and more hostile cultural environment. The laity are waking to their own calling. They are beginning to see out of the custodial box. And laity are questioning the proper role of the church's leadership. We need, then, to look at what were the pieces of the Reformed structure which need to be rediscovered, refounded, and made a part of the missionally focused *Reformed household* which we are seeking to architect for 2020.

GOD'S INITIATIVE FROM START TO FINISH

As we noted in the last chapter, Generation X is a generation whose total experience will have exacerbated their longing for some sense of meaning, structure, transcendence, and connectedness. It is here that the Reformed household's emphases become intensely germane to the mission of God in this cultural chaos. Contrary to all of the cultural rejection of God, connectedness, and transcendent meaning, the fact that there is a community of folk whose lives and thinking are on an alternative track will be most fascinating and taste whetting.

For instance, you will notice that our *Book of Order* sees the particular stance of the Reformed tradition as somehow flowing out of our affirmation of "the majesty, holiness, and providence of God who creates, sustains, rules, and redeems the world in the freedom of sovereign righteousness and love" (G–2.0500). It is that sense of God's saving design that comes through so clearly in the massive teaching of the New Testament under the rubric of "the gospel of the kingdom" (or dominion or sovereign reign) of God. Note, it is *joyous news*, i.e., gospel.

That very sovereign reign of God is the reality, the major structural piece, that needs to be reclaimed in our quest for a viable missionary movement into the twenty-first century. But that will involve us in several other structural pieces that we need to rediscover and refound in the blueprint for our *Reformed household*. Let's settle on these structural pieces, all of which are symbiotically interconnected, so that they are all involved in each other.

1. The whole *predestination* thing needs to be rescued from the grotesque misuses it has undergone and restated in terms that have to do with God's missionary design, so clearly set forth in scripture.
2. The idea of our involvement (or membership or *election*) needs to be looked at also in terms of our participation in God's good purpose in Christ. This will rather drastically reshape the idea of church membership.
3. With the whole Enlightenment enterprise and its confidence in human progress now crumbling and becoming replaced with cultural cynicism, we need to take a fresh look at the realities of the dominion of darkness, the age of this cosmos (the "τον αιωνα του κοσμου τουτου" of Eph. 2:2), into which God's joyous news comes in Christ. The Reformed tradition's sense of the radical falleness and of humankind's proclivity to idolatry, needs to be given a fresh face.
4. Presbyterians get a lot of ribbing over our fetish for *decency and order* in the Christian community, but we need to come clear on the necessity of a community that is ordered to enhance, encourage, support, and give agency to God's mission in Christ. What is its purpose? Who are its leaders? How are the gifts of the Spirit acknowledged in its missionary purpose in the world? This will take some reforming also.
5. The fact that Reformed Christians have always put a premium on the *use of the mind in the service of God* becomes the more urgent in a context of so much mindless evangelicalism and cultural subjectivism. But it needs to be reclaimed within the larger disciplines of Christian discipleship and the whole design of God for our lives which is called *sanctification*.
6. Finally, we will need to look at the larger missional implications our *stewardship* of all of God's creation, as well as of the gospel, our influence, and our resources.

These are six major areas in which Reformed Christians have always had a unique contribution to make to the rest of the people of God. They have been neglected, obscured, forgotten, and generally covered over so much that they are unrecognized by contemporary Presbyterian folk. But they are critical for our mission in the year 2020.

I. LET'S BEGIN WITH PREDESTINATION (AND ALL OF THAT)

Predestined to the Mission of God

There is no place where this old house has so demonstrated the calamity that comes when theology is detached from mission, as in its skewing of the whole concept of predestination, election, and their kindred concepts.[8] This is one of the dark sides of our Reformed history, what with all of the hopeless and embarrassing debates having to do with who is and who is not among the predestined. Alas! There is, of course, that whole area of mystery where God's agency interacts with the human scene. The very idea that God "intruded" into the arena of human autonomy was, to be sure, an affront to modernity.

As we proceed to the *refounding* of the church for the twenty-first century, we are compelled to confess that the whole myth of human autonomy and unending human progress, which was so much at the heart of modernity, has proven to be a dry well that has brought in its wake confusion and despair in the emerging Generation X.

Conversely, the church's belief in the sovereignty and good purpose of God in Jesus Christ is at the heart of a beautiful piece of biblical teaching that gives us hope even where everything is humanly hopeless. That teaching is the missionary concept of predestination, . . . and that is exactly what it is all about. From scripture there are some things that are unmistakably predestined, which we know about and which give context to our lives.

What is predestined (that we *do* know about) is:

- the ultimate demonstration of the glory of God in the whole of creation;
- the blessing of all the nations of the earth through the seed of Abraham, as the early evidence of God's missionary intention toward his creation;
- the election of Israel as an instrument of that mission purpose, as they were called to be a holy nation and a kingdom of priests among the nations of the earth;
- the establishment of the throne of David as eternal (as obscure and unlikely as that seemed in the later pre-Christian centuries);
- the coming of a Messiah and the return of the quenched Spirit (as prophesied in the later pre-Christian centuries) and the manifest reign of Yahweh, with the blessings thereof.

What is predestined is:

- Jesus, as the eternal Son, savior, Word, Messiah, and Lamb of God who takes away the sins of the world, . . . and in whose Lordship the promise of the throne of David is fulfilled and through whom the eternal reign of God (the kingdom of God) is inaugurated;
- the Church as the elect nation, the missionary community being built by Christ to herald his salvation and dominion-new creation;
- the Spirit of the Father and the Son, who is the agent of New Creation, whose role it is to create the Church;

- the preaching of the joyous news of the kingdom of God to all the earth as a witness;
- making disciples among all of the nations, the creation of a people who know and live Christ's teachings and who demonstrate his saving authority;
- the preaching of the cross, the "foolishness of the gospel" of Christ crucified, as the means by which men and women are called into Christ's new creation;
- the inscrutable command to, mystery of, and efficacy of prayer (also so seemingly foolish) through which the sovereign purpose of God is called forth by his people in their new lives in the Spirit as they sojourn through this present age;
- God's purpose, so humanly ridiculous, to use the foolish, the weak, and the "no account" of this world, who love and obey him, to be those who put human confidence in wisdom, power, and prestige in its true light;
- the infinite love of God as a constant which energizes and sustains God's missionary people when all hell breaks loose;
- the reality that finally every knee shall bow and every tongue confess that Jesus Christ is Lord; that the day shall come when all things shall be made new and when the nations shall walk in the light of the Almighty and of the Lamb; and that the kings of the earth shall bring their glory into the city of God, and there shall be no night there;
- that when men and women hear the Word of Christ, when (in the mystery of God's working) their eyes are opened and their ears made to hear, and when they heed Christ's invitation to "Follow me" and turn from their lives of attempted autonomy and darkness to trust in his good news of God's love and purpose—then there is a whole new dimension of life in God's New Creation;
- God's divine power that has given us everything we need for life and godliness through our knowledge of him, who called us by his own glory and goodness. Through these gifts he has given us his very great and precious promises, so that through them we may participate in his divine nature and escape the corruption in the world caused by evil desires (2 Peter 1:3–4);
- the fulfillment of Christ's mandate to his Church: "All authority in heaven and earth has been given to me. Therefore go and make disciples of all nations, baptizing them in the name of the Father and of the Son and of the Holy Spirit, and teaching them to obey everything I have commanded you. And surely I will be with you always, to the very end of the age" (Matt. 28:18–20).

These are at least some of the dimensions of predestination that are not at all in question in our apostolic faith. When Paul gets to the subject of predestination

(Rom. 8), the context is that of a people who love God and so are called to this obvious missionary purpose (the love for God and the calling to his purpose are flip sides of each other). The context is also a church living in dangerous, often nightmarish, conflict with the forces of darkness in local society and in the political empire of Rome. The very notion of predestination is to assure them that their love for God and faith in Jesus Christ means that they are participants in what is *really* going on in human history. It is a word to give heart and hope in their role as pilgrims and strangers as they obey their missionary mandate. It is an encouragement to "hang tough" when everything doesn't fit or is abysmally hostile.

In the almost parenthetical chapters 9, 10, and 11 of Romans, Paul simply lifts the enigma of God's calling of Israel to be a missionary people—a calling they forgot or abandoned. In all of the fascinating discourse, Paul himself appears to be undecided except that somehow God has not abandoned the ultimate purpose for which he called Israel, and that the Gentiles should learn from Israel that they could also forsake their calling. But when he comes to the end of this parenthesis, he both bows in adoration and lays his hand upon his mouth in agnostic humility asking, "Who has known the mind of the Lord?"

Likewise, after trying to explain what is unexplainable about the whole teaching of predestination (unconvincingly), the Westminster Confession at least concludes "So shall this doctrine afford matter of praise, reverence, and admiration of God; and of humility, diligence, and abundant consolation to all that sincerely obey the gospel" (*Book of Confessions*, 6.021).

At the heart of this biblical teaching is the heart of the gospel of God, and its irresistible triumph, even though the conflict in this age will be perennial and intense. The calling is to be part of this missionary purpose, and to confirm your calling and election (2 Peter 1:10) is to be zealous in responding to the eternal kingdom of our Lord and Savior Jesus Christ. These are the *predestined* concepts that must determine the church in its missionary future into the twenty-first century. This *refounded* Reformed household must be put together to be a *Community of the New Creation* which demonstrates and communicates a very genuine experience of the living and thinking of the people of the reign of God.

At the same time, in our *refounding* we must rediscover and reclaim the reality that such a community must be one which holds the faith of Jesus Christ not just in word, but in demonstration of the Holy Spirit and power (1 Cor. 2:4). It is the working of the Holy Spirit to actually create the church. The Spirit gives gifts to enable it to function. The Spirit witnesses to the reality of the reign of God in Christ. The Spirit enables prayer and worship. The *Community in the Spirit* experiences that which eye has not seen nor ear heard.

In this community, the life of the mind and the life in the Spirit are all of a piece. It is essential that this God-given dimension of our life together not be relegated to obscurity, as so much of the church in the modern era relegated it.[9] "The Spirit . . . was not lost after Pentecost."

Now we need to look at some dimensions of this missional community as it is *refounded* to be effective in reaching our Generation X friends.

II. ELECTION: BEYOND MEMBERSHIP TO DISCIPLESHIP

First of all, such a teaching (predestination and election) fairly demolishes the whole contemporary notion of church membership.[10]

This fairly passive and dependent concept of "membership" has been espoused through so much of the custodial history of the church.[11] It fairly misses the whole point of the New Testament teaching about God's calling into the Community of the New Creation. The Romans 8:28–29 reference to predestination says that this initiative of God is for the explicit purpose of conforming men and women to the likeness of his Son. And just what does that mean or look like? Well, there are several dimensions of this conformity that must be in our purview here. One is that the New Testament teaching of our conformity to the *image of God* (or God's Son) has several definable elements to it. None of these have any place for a discipleship that is floating in ecclesiastical passivity, unaccountable or irresponsible. In one passage (Eph. 4:24) believers are exhorted to "put on the new self, created to be like God in *true righteousness and holiness*" [italics mine]. In another (Col. 3:10) believers are told to "put on the new self, which is being *renewed in knowledge* in the image of its Creator" [italics mine].

Put together, these three dimensions of the image of God point us to the character of New Creation persons. They are, like Jesus, living *in synch* with the nature and will of God (holiness); living out the divine intent for justice and righteousness in their human and social relationships (i.e., living out the principles of the Torah); and living out their lives informed by their understanding of who God is, what God is like, and what God's purpose for his own creation and for their missionary incarnations are all about. In essence, they define our missionary character in the world. They define the integrity of the disciple, who then can be an agent of Jesus' mandate, "As the Father has sent me, even so do I send you."

The scriptures teach that to be predestined is to be a self-conscious part of God's missionary purpose in the world. This is our calling, and for this we are both responsible and accountable to the community of disciples—the church.

But, secondly, for our Generation X that has been described as cynical, discontinuous, disconnected, and disposable, such a teaching gives significance to life. It gives meaning to daily existence. It gives an explanation of the ongoing expressions of darkness and a sense of past and future. It is a message of hope in a generation of hopelessness (which is postmodernity's dismal legacy to Generation X). Thirdly, it liberates the laity from the notion of second-class citizenship in the church and exalts them to their role as significant agents in God's unfolding New Creation.

III. SIN, FALLENESS, IDOLATRY, AND THE CULTURAL CONTEXT OF OUR MISSION

Generation X is a product of a culture that is the expression of such forces that are cut off from any roots in the cultural expressions of Christian faith, of a church that has been subverted by the darkness, which has too much become the religious expression of that darkness with its idolatries.[12]

We've covered this somewhat adequately in chapter 2, "Mission: Where the Darkness is the Greatest." At the same time, we are continually brainwashed with the idea that the whole of this life and world are either neutral, in a state of growing perfection (modernity), or somewhat disconnected and meaningless, except as we locally construct some purpose (postmodernity). Reformed Christians have also generally forgotten that Calvin had a "thing" about the human proclivity to idolatry. The Enlightenment and Protestant Liberalism pooh-poohed the whole idea of Satan and the demonic elements in this human scene. But as that modern illusion began to come unraveled, studies have been emerging to reinforce Calvin's thesis. There are, in fact, those institutions that take on a life of their own and an idolatry of themselves, and so become "principalities and powers." These may be any one of a number of institutions, governments, or corporations which begin with valid goals but then succumb to the darkness.

It is easy to read of kings and empires which sought divine status. It is quite another to see the same quest for such status in the company we work for, the country we live in, or the association, party, or union to which we belong. It is true of economic and political and social systems. They may have a very good and legitimate reason for coming into being, but then get inflated estimates of themselves and begin to demand loyalties, values, and devotion which only belong to God.

There are also the irrational "spirits" that seem to filter into culture. We call them *zeitgeists*, plausibility structures, or the dominant social order. Whatever the name, they are real expressions of society and culture that seek to displace God as God. They also put principles influenced by their own self-interest and greed, which are dehumanizing, destructive, and discouraging, in the place of scripture. They are also very volatile, explosive, and destructive when exposed or challenged. Government, media, constitutional rights, economic systems, political parties, freedom of expression, military priorities, college loyalty, and even ecclesiastical institutions can fall into this trap and become "demonic," i.e., destructive and exploitive.

It is such evidences of the falleness and the idolatries of this culture which just may be the most difficult and sinister of our missionary confrontation. The Beast always makes war on the Lamb and his followers. Don't forget it.

So we move on to the *refounding* of a church that is the demonstration of New Creation.

IV. THE CHURCH AS A DISCIPLINED MISSIONARY COMMUNITY

For starters, the form of the *refounded* Reformed household will necessitate a missional presupposition and will require a large and accepting threshold, or front porch.[13] We will be dealing with a whole new generation for whom all of the traditions of the church are, in a word, "weird." Our forms and disciplines will need to be directed at bringing such "outsiders" sensitively into the household of faith. Decency and order are going to have to take on a compassionate missionary role.

Generation X'ers have been deprived of so many pieces of human community that they are left with huge inexplicable vacuums in their lives. One of these is the loss of community and intimacy. Being the children of so many divorced, preoccupied, or abusive homes, they have been left to be formed by impersonal forces, devoid of larger structure. Another loss that flows out of that is the larger purpose of the community of humankind. It is our confessional understanding of the church as the "communion of the saints" that will come as a stream of living water to these thirsty friends.

Since the two wrong turns (mentioned above) of *Constantianization* and the notion of a *custodial* church, the focus was shifted to the institution, buildings, impersonal form, and professional clergy. The Reformed tradition has made a specific point of the necessity for order in the church, but that also has often become an end in itself and has mired (if not taken captive) the church in its institutional minutiae. So much is this true that we have been comically lampooned for our fetish for *decency and order*. The New Testament teachings about the church only make sense when the church is seen in its missionary incarnation.

The church in 2020 will require the implementation of our "church reformed and ever reforming" principle so that we dispense with huge organizational expressions that do not give dynamic expression to the missionary calling of the church. The Great Commission (Matt. 28 version) spells out that the task of the infant church is to (1) make disciples; (2) baptize them into identity with Father, Son, and Holy Spirit; and (3) teach them to observe, or obey, all that Christ has taught. These three must be taken together and not in isolation from each other. Whatever form the church takes to give order to its mission, it must have these components very prominent in it all.

Here are some of the pieces of this that will need refounding for 2020.

The Concept of Discipleship Replacing Membership

When Jesus told his own to "make disciples," he didn't define it for them, but he had demonstrated it. He was in essence telling them to go out into the larger world and to do with others what he had done with and to them. He had, in brief, walked among them as a model of what he was talking about. Please notice that this concept of discipleship has individual persons and their unique personalities written all over it. Jesus used all kinds of occasions to communicate what was happening in his person and his presence among these disciples. He summoned them to "Follow me." He took them into a relationship of closeness and intimacy. There he spent significant time with them, teaching them what the Reign of God, the Messianic Kingdom, was all about. He let them get close enough to eavesdrop on his prayer life (cf. John 17). He listened to their questions and misunderstandings. He was gentle with their weaknesses and foibles. He sent them out to try their wings. He called them back and refined them. He was patient with their sometimes obtuseness to the radicalness of what he was talking about. He fielded their questions. And over a period of months, he essentially reproduced himself in them. He made them into disciples. At the heart of this is that he loved them, and out of that love, he "walked" them into the heart of God's missionary purpose into freedom.

Presbyters (Elders and Pastor-Teachers) as Disciple Makers/Mentors

It is interesting that Generation X is not overly impressed with impersonal programs or curricula. What they really want are those genuine persons who can walk with them into newness and growth. They want *mentors*. This is exactly what Jesus was talking about. Inquirers and newly arrived believers have a right to see what New Creation looks like in the flesh and blood of real, sensitive, mature practitioners. They want to spend time with those who take time

to love, demonstrate, teach, listen, and genuinely embrace Jesus Christ and
them.

It is here that the Lord who is the Spirit equips, or gifts, men and women
to be just such persons, i.e., disciple maker/mentors. As the apostles give us
glimpses into the community of faith that is equipped (and gifted) by the Holy
Spirit, this disciple-making role appears to come forth in the gift of *pastor-
teacher* in Ephesians 4. Paul talks about those who equip the people of God for
their mature ministry in the world. What also appears to come out is the role
of presbyter, as the ministry of mentoring-modeling (1 Peter 5), so that God's
people will have demonstrations before them of how the New Creation life is
lived out. This is also portrayed in Paul's letter to Timothy in which bishop-
presbyters are those who are mature in life, relationships, and knowledge of
scripture, and who have good reputations among outsiders and keep their own
family wholesomely, i.e., who are models and teachers of the new life in Christ.

It comes out very clearly in Paul's own teachings about his ministry. He
says with utmost candor, "Follow my example, as I follow the example of
Christ" (1 Cor. 11:1). This, in his mind, seems the same as saying, "Be imita-
tors of God, therefore, as dearly loved children" (Eph. 5:1), or "Whatever you
have learned or received or heard from me, or seen in me—put it into practice. And the God of peace will be with you" (Phil. 4:9). This concept of the
role models, the mentors of the Christian community, the disciple makers, is
obviously the working of the Holy Spirit. These pastor-teachers or presbyters
are those whose ministry is that of conforming the human members of the
community into the likeness of the Son, and therefore making them the
obvious and contagious agents of forming others. It is a ministry that is very
person oriented. It is relational, not only with the others in the community,
but with the Chief Shepherd to whom they are very consciously accountable
(Heb. 13:17; 1 Pet. 5:4).

Somehow in the custodial and institutional distortions within the church,
this key missional principle became obscured. Leader-presbyters have been
(too) frequently chosen and presbyters elected, for all kinds of reasons that
have nothing to do with their obvious lives of contagious holiness, proven
disciple-making skills, and their genuine New Creation character. This same
unintended distortion carries over into the concept of clergy and seminaries
that make the rite of ordination dependent on willingness and academic skills,
but seldom on the track record of fruitful disciple-making within a Christian
community. What this has meant, of course, is that quite frequently the real
disciple makers are the laypeople who are actually being conformed to the likeness of God's Son and who are reproducing that likeness in others by their
genuine and faithful lives. This often makes the clergy irrelevant.[14]

Smaller Groups of Intimacy as Surrogate Families of Faith

A generation so disconnected from wholesome relationships of genuineness, love, intimacy, caring, and conversation leave our X'er friends incapable of so much of the redeemed society that is part of our gospel. The large congregations, organized impersonally where one can participate in anonymity, simply will not cut it with such a generation. The church in the year 2020 may well have a larger expression, but the working heart of its missionary incarnation is going to be smaller house churches or accountability groups, where we are known as persons, where we share some responsibility for others, and where we are accountable for our lives and behaviors as brothers and sisters in Christ. In other words, there will be a critical place for a relational context where persons meet in faith, hope, love, and mutual responsibility within the community.

John Wesley saw this critical need in the revival of the eighteenth century. New converts needed a context in which to process their new lives in Christ and to be held accountable and responsible. The Wesleyan "Class Meetings" were the form that met this need. The New Testament church, as we often forget, met primarily in homes, which meant that there were a fairly limited number of folk involved. It is obvious that everybody had names and were known to the others. This stands in stark contrast to the disenchanted young adult who exploded in my Presbyterian face, "How can I submit myself to elders who don't even know my name?"

How many hundreds and thousands of persons are "lost" on the church rolls in the Presbyterian family because they were never organically integrated into any small community of faith where they were taken seriously and held accountable? Such smaller communities will be a *sine qua non* of our church in 2020.

V. MINDS AND HEARTS IN THE SERVICE OF GOD

There has been an inordinate amount of mindlessness in the Presbyterian Church in the latter part of the twentieth century. We have spent billions of dollars on superbly equipped educational buildings, and we have succeeded in producing, according to the Presbyterian Poll, a distressing generation of dysfunctional and biblically illiterate Presbyterian folk. Even the much publicized "evangelical" wing of the church in the United States comes under scathing criticism—"The scandal of the evangelical mind is that there is not much of an evangelical mind."[15]

Now we're facing Generation X who are completely detached from any semblance of Christian understanding. And as we *refound* the Reformed household to be a missional community to reach these men and women, we're going to have to begin with the reality that they are coming from "nowhere," for such is the legacy of postmodernism. Not only that, but they are coming, too often, with all of their broken relationships, confusion, bewilderment, abuse, brilliant minds, cynicism, and hopelessness. We begin there.

The Reformed expression of Christian faith has always (in principle) put a premium on the use of the mind in the service of God.[16] To be renewed in knowledge, as we have seen, is a clear expression of the image of God in the people of the New Creation. But such knowledge can easily become dead-ended obsession with intelligence. That "truth is in order to goodness" is also a clarion Reformed principle (cf. G–1.0304). At the same time, so much of the church's life has been wrapped up in a notion of "Christian education" that has, again, been far too much Christian entertainment or activities that have had no clear focus on discipleship or equipping for mission as exiles and aliens in a strange world. The church in 2020 will not be able to indulge such distractions. Likewise, the quest for "meaningful" and "inspirational" preaching produced a biblically illiterate church in the twentieth century, alas.

Put positively, the missionary context of 2020 is going to rather drastically redefine the ministry of both the pastor-teacher and the others equipping ministries in the community of faith. Generation X, I think, will not allow for mindlessness. Nor will they be content with abstractions. Here are the laity, who constitute 95-plus percent of the church and who live 160-plus hours of the week, not in Christian community, but in missionary engagement with the realities of the neo-pagan society. This means that they are called to live out their New Creation lives in the midst of alien company policies or restraints of the system that forbid them to express any Christian theistic principle. They encounter the policies of greed and destructiveness in politics and the economy. They may live in sterile and depersonalized residential neighborhoods or in neighborhoods infested with evidences of darkness. They have social and professional friends in neighborhoods and workplaces who may be other X'ers looking for hope or who may be adherents of other religions.

The Reformed household is going to be the setting in which these men and women have time to process their lives in the light of scripture, where mind and Spirit come together. The household will be the place where a few hours together with other aliens and pilgrims can sort out the engagement between the dominion of darkness and the dominion of light. It will be the context in which they can honestly discuss their lives, in which they can pray and worship and study together about their transformational and redemptive calling. These intellectual and ethical and theological realities are complex. How do I love my neighbor and somehow incarnate God's design in the midst of the imperfect and tragic? How do I see God's common grace at work in non-Christian people and settings? How do I practice the New Creation life in all of the dimensions of my life? Lesslie Newbigin speaks of this new community as the "hermeneutic of the gospel," i.e., that community which interprets the gospel to the watching world. He states, among other things that,

> . . . it will be a community where men and women are prepared for and sustained in the exercise of the priesthood in the world.[17]

Even the congregation's worship will be part of this. No longer just an "Order of Worship" conceived in abstraction to fulfill some denominational liturgical guide. No. Rather, it will be the time when the family of God reflects on God and his Word on the sovereign good purpose of God and his power at work. Worship will have to be an expression of Spirit and of mind in missionary preparation of the people of God, the laity, and for their 160 hours of missionary incarnation. Pastor-teachers will be instrumental in creating a community where the Word of God dwells richly, and where scriptures are dealt with seriously in depth and application.

VI. STEWARDSHIP AS A MISSIONARY CONCEPT

As the X'er men and women are formed by a dynamic concept of "the already but not yet kingdom of God" (the understanding that they have been called into God's missionary purpose for the world), they will realize that two realities exist co-terminously which are opposed to each other, and they will become aware of the realities or dominions in which they live. It will also make them quite aware of how the destructiveness of so much previous economic and social policy has left them facing nearly intractable problems. The cultural and social neighborhood in which they live will be a challenge which will tax them, and it will call forth all of their New Creation sense of imagination and purpose.

The stewardship of all of life[18] will involve them in confronting redemptively the issues of urban decay, economic greed, political process, moral darkness, and eroded relationships on a local and international scale. The Christian community will no longer be able to coast along in passive indifference to the personal and cultural darkness of the local and larger "neighborhood" in which the church exists. Stewardship will no longer be some minimal look at tithing of time, talents, and money, as it was for so long. Rather, it will encompass the use of every expression and influence of the individual members and the larger Christian community in the sovereign good purpose of God to glorify his name in the totality of his subverted creation. Such stewardship will put the church in costly missionary confrontation with entrenched and sophisticated powers hostile to any such redemptive stewardship.

Such missionary stewardship will not be abstract but rather incarnational. The love and grace of God toward his creation will be accompanied by the Christian communities' serious involvement. Such involvement will include making its residence in the place of greatest need and seeking the redemptive solutions for the whole of God's blighted creation. Christians will find co-belligerents who, by God's common and preserving grace, share their concerns in many areas and will join Christians in accomplishing mutual goals for the common purpose. It is obvious that the place of the Reformed household with its keen sense of this wholistic stewardship will give content to the five concerns above. This will be especially true in the support and prayer, joined with grappling the depths of the issues confronted. Superficial piety and devotional detachment won't hack it.

What is encouraging about the X'ers is that they are pragmatic and entrepreneurial by nature. Given the vision and sense of God's sovereign purpose and calling, given the *weltanschauung,* they will rearrange the ecclesiastical furniture in nurture and worship to make the community effective, flexible, informed, and cooperatively present as agents of the New Creation. Huge amounts of the institutional baggage inherited with the church from their Boomer parents will be consigned to the "who needs it?" category, as the X'ers construct an ecclesiastical wineskin in which the transformational vigor of the Reformed principles will have their fullest effect. Worship and study will be much more participatory. But always before X'ers will be the missionary goal of their calling. This will determine what becomes part of their lives together as the community of the New Creation.

This *Blueprint* will be always in process, but the post-denominational Christian community will be formed with some of these realities in place. It will have its roots in the valid traditions of the past, but it will not look much like the church it inherited from the twentieth century.

A SPIRIT MOVEMENT (RATHER THAN A DENOMINATION)

Denominations are confusing the X'ers, and they will be increasingly ignored by the year 2020. There will be remnants and shadows of denominations, but the boundaries will be much more indistinct. One can argue that denominations are a product of the modern era, or that they are "the moral failure of Christianity" (R. Niebuhr), or none of the above. Such institutions, as someone said, are "probably necessary, but not always helpful." They have had their role in the providence of God. Unfortunately, they usually institutionalized some particular doctrine or expression of the church, and so became provincial, denying the diversity of gifts as well as catholicity. They did give some structure to the missionary movement of the church and there will continue to be the need for structures, accountability, and supportive community.

At the same time, in 2020 the climate will not allow the exclusiveness and institutional loyalties that were engendered by denominations (even unto bloodshed) in the modern era.

But a *movement*, ah, there is something else. As Jesus Christ builds his Church in human history, movements energized by the Holy Spirit can call forth all kinds of holy laughter. Movements are not predictable nor containable. When the church becomes too institutionalized or distracted or forgetful to be a viable wineskin for mission—count on it, a movement will arise. Movements are focused, creative, rambunctious, and have a playful way of leaping over traditional (and denominational) boundaries. Movements are creative and versatile. They are highly motivated and focused on specific goals. Movements create new structures, and reenergize and refound old ones. In a very real sense, the history of movements within the Christian church indicate that they are spontaneous and often out of any human control. This means that movements are not always neat. Actually, they can be disruptive and messy.

But Spirit movements break the church free to invite the Savior back into table fellowship and to engage in new and costly lives of discipleship and obedience in new and fruitful ways. Jesus taught us the lesson. New wine needs wineskins supple enough to contain the ferment and life of the wine. So it is with the church. It is called forth by the sovereign Lord Jesus to be a missionary community, and it must remain flexible enough to be just that. When the church ossifies, or becomes too rigid to be free for missionary engagement in the world, the Creator Spirit calls individuals and groups to become pathfinders into a new movement of faith and obedience.

By the year 2020, Generation X will have discovered that the beauty and genius of the former Presbyterian Church was not its form of government but its theology and mission. The Spirit will have energized a rediscovery of this, and a movement will begin to develop around this to meet the spiritual hungerings and wanderings of postmodern men and women. After decades of mindlessness, the massive biblical and theological thinking that frees and transforms will have been delivered out of its captivity to *academe*. It will begin to take on momentum as it unexpectedly moves down to the daily lives of laymen and laywomen in the homes, offices, side-streets, and gatherings of the Christian community. The movement will not be simply a matter of dispassionate doctrine either.

This movement will have begun as one individual here and another there rediscovers the treasure. A group of students and/or a few faculty in a seminary will have ignited a whole new Reformed and evangelical (tie those two words together) awakening. Sessions of struggling Presbyterian Churches, sobered by their immanent demise and weary of bland and unfocused religious gobbledegook will wake up to what is already their heritage and their mission. Networks between these awakened entities will develop in the providence of God. The Breath of Life will energize a new look at scriptures and at all of life with eyes that had long been closed. The movement will spill over into class meetings and small groups of other Christian traditions and will interact with them in mutual discovery. Appetites will be whetted, and a new genre of Reformed resources will come forth to equip the movement.

A study center here or a theological conference there will play a part. Cultural and social challenges will provoke new missionary engagement with the world. The children of Generation X will be even more brutally honest than their parents and will become swept up in the movement. They will gather in conferences and retreats, looking at the context of their lives and becoming the catalysts for an even more creative Reformed movement. Teams of energized laity, formed by such a Reformed *weltanschauung*, will spread the contagion as they travel from church to church. Clergy and seminaries will have been bypassed; they will wake up to the fact that they are archaic and no longer relevant to the church, and they will be swept up into the movement with new focus and purpose. Reformed resources on tapes, videos, CD ROMS, or on web sites and computer networks will play their part.

Be on the lookout for something like temporary Reformed households, or "floating parishes" that will arise to meet needs and then merge into other Christian community structures. This will drive old-line church functionaries and bureaucrats bonkers. But our belief is that the sovereign God wills his own glory, and his sovereign good purpose will be accomplished. Our God also makes us look at cultural darkness with the anticipation of a "lookout." The Breath of God blows upon the inarticulate hungerings of God's unsuspecting saints; our movement will get totally out of human control, and rivers of life will flow back into moribund churches and institutions. God is not limited by human control mechanisms. This movement will not only be an intentionally *missionary* movement, but it will also be an intentionally *subversive* movement whose goal will be to communicate the glory of God into all of the structures and communities of God's church and creation. And its life and power will be a demonstration of the Holy Spirit. Count on it.

THE ONGOING ARCHITECTURAL TASK

At the beginning of this attempt to provide a blueprint for the twenty-first century, I confessed that it would be foolish to attempt such. There are so many unknowns before us. The wonderful left-handed providences of the sovereign God that break in and break out of our human designs always keep us both expectant and humbled. Add to this the fact that there is no *generic* Presbyterian community. There are always the vicissitudes of time, place, personnel, cultural tides, and crises. But what I have provided are some major suggestions and proven structural pieces. What is required now is "energy, intelligence, *imagination* [italics mine], and love" called for in our leadership in the *Book of Order*, G-14.0405 (8). We face a new and unexplored mission field. It is not for the timid or unbelieving. Humanly, it is intimidating if not frightening. But with the God whom we worship and serve, it is fraught with hope and joy and fruitfulness. The foundation is laid in Jesus Christ. What is required now are skilled master builders.

Veni Creator Spiritus.

8

In Retrospect
From the Year 2020

JANUARY 15, 2020: OUR *BLUEPRINT* FOR THE TWENTY-FIRST century was begun a few years before the end of the last (twentieth) century. It turned out to be more than a little prophetic. Each passing year, as the culture changed drastically, the PC(USA)'s assumption that it would continue to survive, invulnerable, in patterns accumulated over many previous decades proved to be ill-founded. Each year provided more and more disenchantment with any call for, or interest in, denominational loyalty. The spiritual hungerings of the younger generations and their near total paganization made them indifferent to all such denominational labels. All of this we anticipated in our *Blueprint*. More than two decades have now passed, and the scene in 2020 is wildly different and exciting, not to mention much more difficult and challenging. We need to look back in retrospect and record some of the things that have brought us to this point.

From this present vantage point, probably the most catalytic events were some decisions made by the church's governing bodies in those closing years of the century. Those decisions revealed how deep and wide was the fault line between (1) those parts of the church who took seriously their scriptural, Christ-o-centric, and Reformed (confessional) convictions on the one hand, and (2) those, on the other hand, who were more fascinated with the church's polity and institutional existence, but were rather casual (if not forgetful) about both the God-given mission and the theological content of that mission. This second group is both tragic and difficult to explain. Part of it was the product of that (how to say it?) *pious agnosticism* which was the fruit of the

118

Enlightenment-Modern-Liberal philosophies and theologies that had been quite prominent in the academies for many years. Those folk had a quite different worldview (*weltanschauung*) from their (Reformed) and evangelical counterparts. Some probably just drifted along with the popular currents as the church sought relevancy, inclusiveness, and acceptance in an increasingly neo-pagan society. Whatever the reason, the two general constituencies discovered in the debates that they had no common language of discourse. They stood on different tectonic plates of faith and understanding. Historians will try to explain all of this sometime in the years to come. We simply note it here and leave it for future scholars.

No schism took place. There was no traumatic ecclesiastical rupture. It was more like an amicable and quiet divorce. Those who were to become our present (Reformed) communities simply realized that it was poor stewardship to seek to maintain the archaic denominational wineskins. The reasoning was that those structures continued to drain huge resources, but for the most part, did not seem at all realistic about drastic cultural changes. They were more than a little indifferent to both the theology and the mission for which the Presbyterian Church had been founded (according to its constitutional documents). In some ways (to use another metaphor), it was something like passive euthanasia, i.e., it was simply allowed to end in the form to which it had come. What was moribund was quietly allowed to come to a fitting end. And so it happened.

Those persons across the fault line sought frantically to preserve it in its previous form. After all, its existence was their primary *raison d'être*. Shadowy remnants of that previous form are still around to this day. At the same time, they have dwindled and become more and more irrelevant. That remnant has gradually faded to the margins of any significance. Those parts of the former Presbyterian structures which had true viability, however, and were engaged in common mission with the (Reformed) communities, took on new life, creativity, and fruitfulness.

AN INCREASINGLY DIFFICULT CULTURAL CONTEXT

In these intervening decades, the context of the Christian mission has shifted and changed in ways almost unimaginable twenty-five years ago. The vigor within the Christian world shifted from the West to a vigorous church in the East and the Southern hemisphere. The erosion, caused by North America's endemic secular materialism and greed, laid bare the tragic failure of the North American Christian community to influence the behavior of its members at a basic level. The neo-pagan darkness exhibited itself, among other things, in the ebbing of public acceptance of the Christian institutions. Church giving and church property were subjected to increasing taxation. The Christian mission had to divest itself of many of its luxuries, unneeded and unused structures, staff, real estate, and organizational nonessentials. The darkness also expressed more and more (usually) passive hostility to any public Christian expressions.

The up side of all of this was a sifting and a refining within the Christian community. Christian people demanded of the church that it be both more articulate in, and demonstrative of, its message. It became more and more difficult to lure people into membership of existing churches which were simply enclaves of traditional religion. The *Generation X'ers* proved themselves every bit as pragmatic, skeptical, and entrepreneurial as we had prophesied. The *Millennial Generation*, just behind the X'ers, were even more confrontational (in-your-face) with their honest demands. They asked the right questions. They insisted upon examples of demonstrated discipleship. They constructively questioned and challenged traditions that had no obvious relationship to the message. They were more than a little impatient with church institutions. Churches which expected loyalty—but which did not conversely provide ministry to equip them to deal with life, nor create true Christian community—were given short shrift.

X'ers also were much more conscious of their need for the power of the transcendent God in their lives. They were thereby much more open to the energizing and expression of the Holy Spirit in the realities of their lives. Congregational life became more disciplined and more expectant of the power of God. In short, the encroaching darkness of these recent decades has produced an awakening, . . . a *revival* if you will.

WILD AND FREE (AND REFORMED)

Before we record the history of these past couple of decades any further, there are several points which we need to explain in order to get us from the thesis of *Blueprint 21* to the present. The first point is that, early on, the vital congregations which emerged out of the chaos at the turn of the century simply ceased using the name *Presbyterian*. The reason was quite simple; that name communicated no meaning and no importance to anybody. Zip. It was even a stumbling block since it communicated not a thing to outsiders. Add to this the fact that those outsiders looking for God did not find their way into a particular congregation because of some way it organized its inner life (presbyters, and all of that).

The second point is a similar one, and has to do with the term *Reformed*. The term has enormous meaning and content for some as a historical designation for a particular understanding of the Christian faith. Throughout our blueprint we have talked about a "Reformed household for *Generation X*." But the reality is that the designation is never used today to describe the church (even though its Reformed content may be very visible). So from this point on, in our retrospect, we'll put that word in parentheses, just so that we'll remember that Reformed is still what we're talking about for those few who remember.

The purpose of our *Blueprint 21* was to look at the then (c. 2000) struggling Presbyterian family, and to see what there was in its life and history that was so valuable to the whole of the Body of Christ, to "the one holy catholic and apostolic church" that it needed to be saved. What was its founding genius that needed to be *refounded*? What needed to be a part of the larger church's life of faith and mission in the twenty-first century? We lifted up three components[1] that would be essentials to such refounding and viability, as the cultural setting became more pagan and even more hostile. Yet in our wildest imagination, we never could have foreseen what has actually taken place in the intervening years. The principles and prognostications of that blueprint have, for the most part, been amazingly realized. They have done so far beyond anything we could ever, ever have conceived at that point, "far more abundantly than all we ask or imagine, . . . to him be glory . . ." (Eph. 3:20–21).

The much parodied *decency and order* description so often hung on the old Presbyterians in mocking humor took on an entirely new and liberated connotation. Far from being an excuse for stodginess, formality, and stifling control, those words became (as with the Corinthian church of the New Testament) an absolutely necessary principle of wholesome discipline and order in a church that had become rambunctiously alive, creative, fruitful, and energized. Discipline and form were necessary to keep it from self-destructing out of sheer unbridled enthusiasm. Adventuresomeness and holy obedience met in a new wave of transforming mission. Who would have ever thought it?

An eminent and venerable church leader by the name of John Mackay said in the middle of the last century that he would not be surprised if the church of the future belonged to "a reformed Catholicism, or a matured Pentecostalism—or a combination of the two." Dr. Mackay was prophetic beyond his imagination also. What has taken place in these two decades of the twenty-first century is something like that. Only it is a *liberated* (Reformed) awareness of the implications of the sovereignty and majesty of God, along with a matured (chastened?) and wholesome Pentecostalism (they go together, actually). The sovereign God, the holy God "who creates, sustains, rules and redeems the world in his righteousness and love,"[2] whom those Presbyterians of the twentieth century professed to believe, proved that such a God could not be taken captive, tamed, or frustrated in his own sovereign good purpose. It was more than an little humorous.

The Spirit of God, the Holy Spirit, in that same sovereign freedom and love, came blowing as a cleansing Fire and a life-giving Wind upon that Presbyterian chaos. The Breath of God came in the most unlikely and unexpected places and times. After generations of theological and ecclesiastical *hubris*, intellectual pride, numerical decline, not to mention an abundance of seminary degrees granted, what do you think? A new phenomenon surprised the somnolent Presbyterian remnant. At first it appeared in small and isolated trickles, then as a rushing torrent of awakened men and women with razor sharp minds and flaming hearts. Life. Power. Signs and wonders. Biblical obedience. Unashamed Christians. Huge cultural impact. Conflict with the darkness. Living Water. Suffering. Missionary confrontation with the dominant order. Apostolic evidences as had not even been imagined in generations.

What is more, it became hugely contagious. Freed from all of the confines of former denominational straitjackets, the *refounded (Reformed) household* was a rambunctiously missionary movement. It was so much so that it infiltrated the rest of the Christian Church with its unique gifts, and in turn, was continually enriched by the gifts of other great church traditions. The (Reformed) community put away any remnant of defensiveness and elitism. This was replaced by excited anticipation, freedom, joy, and daily expectation. The sovereign God proved to be alive and well and full of surprises. And this Sovereign God intruded into that unlikely and discouraged scene to demonstrate to them his sovereign dominion (New Creation) in the twenty-first century.

HOW DID ALL OF THIS HAPPEN?

How did all of this happen? Well, frankly, at first it all was sheer *chaos*. Then slowly and with a lot of soul-searching, newness began to dawn. Even though the former PC(USA) had been increasingly troubled and forgetful of its heritage, we need to remember that it had been at the very least a comfort zone to many simply because of its long history. When the events and decisions of the late twentieth century caused it all to begin to unravel, it was painful and chaotic. That was all necessary in hindsight. But there were more than a few casualties. There are some factors, however, which took place humanly (along with the sovereign Breath of God) that can be catalogued.

1. When All Else Fails: Pray

Don't laugh. People do tend to pray in a crisis. Desperation seems to remind people of the ministry of prayer. Maybe it was the increasing presence of the Korean Presbyterians with their profound dependence on prayer within the church. They, at least, were moving into visible leadership, and gave to so many the model of effectual prayer. Or maybe it was the sheer desperation of having all human dependencies and traditional props snatched away. However it came about, there came into being both innumerable focused prayer groups and ministries, along with larger concerts of prayer among godly Presbyterian folk. This all had a centripetal force in that it began to suck more and more people in from the outer edges of the fellowship with greater intensity. Presbyterians were crying out to God, "Help us." They were asking the Sovereign Lord for direction, for power, for the next steps of obedience, and for wisdom. God obviously heard, and in faithfulness, answered. Scriptures came alive with meaning. The newness, life, and clear vision of hope began to emerge in thrilling episodes.

2. An Awakened Laity

The exciting part of this story has to do with the laity. For years there had been a smoldering rebellion brewing among the Presbyterian laity. The gifts and mission of the laity in their daily lives and in their missionary incarnation through the week had, for the most part, been carried on without significant assistance from the clergy. These women and men were (and are) the cutting-edge of the Christian witness in the world. For too long the clergy had created little enclaves for themselves in the churches. These were a kind of sub-culture that were, for the most part, irrelevant to the confrontations, struggles, and missionary engagement in which these laypersons lived. The laity had frankly, and for all practical purposes, allowed the clergy this indulgence. It became more and more apparent, however, that for all of the ordination standards and for all of the theological education that had gone on with these clergy, nothing had been guaranteed. Too much of the Presbyterian Church's descent into chaos was with clergy leadership at the forefront.

But when the whole thing began to come apart, it was these lay disciples of Jesus Christ who were roused to action and leadership. Their enormous gifts, skills, prayers, and studies took them back to the basics to *refound* the (Reformed) household. What happened was that they looked deeply into what had brought this church into being in the first place. They didn't owe anybody anything. They *did* intend to be faithful to God. What they discovered was something nobody had ever bothered to bring to their attention, namely the incredible *weltanschauung* of the (Reformed) faith and life.

It was like *Whoo-ee!* They even discovered that John Calvin actually wrote his *Institutes of the Christian Religion* to equip the emerging middle-class laity in France for their daily life and witness. They became incredibly excited about using every occasion to equip themselves to be a genuinely *New Creation people* and to impact neighbors, neighborhoods, and their daily occupations.

Another serendipity was that as Presbyterian laypersons rediscovered their heritage, they found out that their Wesleyan and Catholic lay friends were also rediscovering their rich heritages, and all of this was shared across lunch tables in innumerable settings with great joy and mutual profit.

3. Refounding of a *Laity-focused* Pastor-Teacher Gift

All of which leads to the next interesting development. All that made up the prevailing concept of "clergy" had become so muddled that these same laity began to look critically at what they needed in order to be well-equipped for their daily encounter with the world. What kind of well-equipped teachers and disciple makers were needed? Then they looked at what they had actually been getting from their pastors.

Again there was pain and dismay. Many very sincere men and women had offered themselves to the church for ministry out of that older pattern of what such ministry involved. They had gone off to seminaries as expected. They were led to believe that the acquisition of a theological degree would surely equip them to be pastors and teachers—leaders of the church. But when they finished this step and got out into pastoral positions, they began to realize how they had been deceived by the system. Frequently they were far less equipped than the laity they were supposed to be equipping.

As the laity asserted themselves and looked into what it would take to equip them for their daily ministries in the workplace and in the realities of a growing darkness, they also looked again into scriptures. What they found was that the laying on of hands (which became our rite of ordination) was conferred upon those who had demonstrated particular gifts *within* the Christian community. Our laymen and laywomen had too often been disappointed by those coming out of the old system. Without any well-defined moment of reaction, our awakening congregations simply began to do it differently. Gifted and proven men and women, who were mature in faith and life and respected by their peers, were literally asked to assume the pastoring and teaching leadership in the community (without seminary degree or ordination).[3]

On the other hand, this move by the laity to refound the pastoral and teaching position through persons who had been in the trenches with them—and whom they knew and respected—was not done in ignorance of its dangers. Nor were the lessons of history unknown to them. These communities of awakened laity realized that those who were to be the communities' teachers really needed to be of well-equipped minds and maturity of life. They needed some ongoing context for sharpening their skills and gifts, as well as interaction with the larger church outside of the congregation. They realized all too well that there was a large mental component in this. How to accomplish this was another of the creative developments.

4. A Pragmatic Approach to Biblical and Theological Excellence

A part of the thrill of rediscovering their heritage was that (Reformed) Christians put a priority on well-equipped minds. The laity who were the leaders of the (Presbyterian) communities were not at all helpless or ill-informed. They were quite accustomed to finding, or developing, resources to accomplish excellence in the many fields in which they operated daily. They were quite adept at resourcing, networking, and developing what was necessary to make things happen in their workplace. They were also very pragmatic, critical, and could be brutally direct when evaluating effectiveness. So the existing structures of theological education took a hit soon after the chaos became obvious. For all of their traditional places of respect in the former church, the seminaries had become too much a scene of theological esoterica and missional indifference. And when it came to equipping the minds of the laity for the missionary challenges outside of the worshipping congregation, the seminaries had been a great disappointment.

As the lay leaders of our awakened communities looked at this, they began to ask, Where are the godly minds and hearts? Where are those who can equip us and our congregational pastors, teachers, and leaders into fruitful life and witness? Where are models of those who really understand the laity's daily mission in the workplace? Who understands the culture in which we live and work? Who has a heart for God? Who has proven gifts in communicating good biblical and theological understanding to folk such as we? Who understands our ethical confrontations as Kingdom citizens? Such questions began to float across e-mail and internet channels. They were traded across tables in meetings and business luncheons. People in the church in Atlanta were in meetings with their counterparts in Seattle or Boston. It didn't take long for all kinds of creative networks to develop.

It also didn't take long for these local leaders to identify those like-minded spirits in academic institutions who had the kind of proven minds and hearts they were looking for. What emerged were numerous *ad hoc* conferences, video and electronic resources, and seminars, as well as intensive courses in non-traditional forms that made accessible to the new pastors and teachers the very best of Christian life and thought. Computer websites put all of this within reach of a new genre of pastor-teacher. These in turn began to skillfully get it into the context of the lives of their friends who had asked them to assume this ministry. A whole new breed of pastor and teacher equipped with *laity eyes* began to form congregations who actually interpreted the gospel to their families, neighbors, workplace associates, and professional colleagues.

5. A Surprising New Order of (Reformed) "Jesuits"

If you think that all of the theological institutions simply withered away, they didn't. At least not all of them did. It took them a while to come to grips with the reality of the chaos, however. Remember that seminaries have trustees. And many of those trustees were the very same laywomen and laymen who had been awakened. Not only that, but many of the faculty had been living in seminaries for years, almost in exile. They had been longing for "the deliverance of Israel" so to speak. They had been caught in a system that was captive to the modern period. The unbelief and agnosticism of academe quenched their spirits. Still they had done their best to be faithful within the often alien situation they inherited along with these institutions.

As the awakened church began to pray, the effect of the prayers began to light fires in the seminaries. The communication between the awakened congregations and the seminaries increased, as did the ministry of the congregations to the faculty and students who were there. To be sure, those institutions which doggedly espoused the old patterns of the twentieth century and the old order declined. About half of the seminaries were ultimately sold off because of lack of support.

Out of this chaos, however, came something totally unexpected and thrilling. In much leaner and more chastened communities of scholarship, and with much more missional eyes, bright young men and women with missionary fervor asserted themselves to be a formative factor in the *refounded household*. What happened was historically reminiscent of the episode of Ignatius Loyola gathering with his friends in prayer, and with missionary vision, determining to win the world for Christ through education. Out of that prayer meeting in the sixteenth century came the Jesuit Order, which is of no small significance in the mission history of the world. This company of our own young men and women with evangelical hearts and exceptional minds began an intense engagement with congregations, laity, culture, and the challenges of social order. This spontaneous movement became a major factor in the awakened (Reformed) household, becoming a powerful missionary community as of this moment. It is important to underscore the fact that this movement is a very *de-clergified* movement. Its purpose is that of a mobile, flexible, and available resource of Christian thinking for the grassroots of the awakened community. Their strategy was to reinhabit the faculties of the remaining colleges and seminaries in order to serve the laity and the congregations.

6. The End of Eurocentricity

It needs to be noted that in these intervening twenty years, the dominance of the Eurocentric culture (especially its British and Scottish expressions) in the United States has simply ceased to be. Not only have there been successive ethnic invasions, predominantly of Asiatics, Hispanics, Africans, and Indians, but there have also come the generational changes we predicted twenty years ago. This has had very marked influence on the life of the church in many ways. From the African Americans came a more participatory and dialogical style of worship. From Korean Presbyterians came the gift of a new emphasis on prayer and on the disciplines of group accountability. From African Christians came a rich sense of tribal responsibility for those human beings in need and for the extended family role of the church in meeting those needs. The younger generations, along with these national and ethnic traditions, brought new music and new expressions of worship.

7. The Metamorphosis of Congregational Life

The church had nearly always been conceived as an institution. In the awakened (Reformed) household, it was much more relational and community focused. The institutional image promoted a significantly depersonalized concept of membership, i.e., members were those loyal to the institution. Members of the younger generation were the products of a culture devoid of intimacy. They required a different quality of Christian community experience. Their lack of any experience of strong family and relational ties demanded a church life that was not even remotely impersonal. All that had preoccupied the former institutional form, i.e., buildings, organizations, programs, and all imper-sonal accoutrements, was intentionally replaced.

What slowly emerged was a community in which every individual has iden-tity. Our churches are formed with flexibility but also with a discipline whereby every participant is accountable to the community's missionary purpose. This is the "up front" commitment of all of those who identify with our (Reformed) households. Persons are attracted by our community's message, life, and vitality. Even more they seem to be attracted by the way our members live and think, which is obviously formed by something utterly different than anything they have known—something wholesome. These persons are welcomed by our community's missionary embrace (cf. below). But once they decide to follow Christ, and become baptized participants, they are not only accountable to each other, but responsible to be a part of the community's life and mission. Our communities are frequently "floating" communities without buildings, or else sharing buildings with other Christian communities. But the organizational, physical, and logistical elements of the community (the wineskins) exist only to implement the mission and the community. Primarily our larger congregational communities are composed of numerous small groups or households which become the primary relationships of intimacy and accountability, as well as nurture and caring.

The new forms of this awakened church are too many to mention. Deliberate tracks of discipleship and Christian formation are not casual. The cultural context is too alien to allow the luxury of activities that go nowhere. Also, membership involves growth in knowledge and in relationships. There is no anonymous or passive-dependent membership in these refounded churches. Every person is a *person*, and every person is a working, functioning part of the community's life and missional responsibility. This contagious life expresses itself in many diverse groups and at odd schedules to meet the demands of a busy and involved membership.

Needless to say, worship is also quite different from that of the last century, but only in its much more participatory style (as noted above). Worship is literally at the heart of the family of God. Worship is spending time together with a focus made possible by adoration. Teaching, in the (Reformed) tradition, is very important. Music is varied. But with the demanding schedules of the vital congregations, there are more than one occasion and more than one form of worship. Time is precious and so worship is very carefully prayed through and sensitively planned. It is, to put it mildly, intense. Those who plan and lead the times of worship do it with much prayer and sensitivity to the realities in which the members live and minister.

8. Cultural Sensitivity and Evangelistic Threshold

One key place where the Presbyterian family of the last century "went to sleep" was in its capacity to understand the context of its life and mission. There was little effort made to keep a keen ear to the ground in terms of the continually changing cultural context as it manifested itself in the lives of those outside the church. What this meant was that the Presbyterian Church became more and more provincial and cut off from the very people on its doorstep. It catered primarily to what it called "Presbyterian-type" people who were familiar with the traditions. Little was done within the Christian congregations to tune in the members to the hearts and thinking of those neighbors who were still outside.

The awakened and refounded (Reformed) household takes very seriously the need for continual *contextualization* and spends serious time listening to the culture around it. Then it uses its best efforts to create bridges that speak to the spiritual hungering of those still in darkness. As the multi-ethnic and multi-religious makeup of the population becomes more inescapable, this means that many of our neighbors are adherents of other religious faiths. This, along with the fact that increasing secularization has created an emptiness and meaninglessness that breeds spiritual darkness and loneliness all around us.

This means that our awakened churches have a very large front (and back) porch for welcoming those spiritually lost and hungry, as well as religiously confused friends who come looking for God (and who come by both the front door and the back door). Our members are sensitized to ministry to the seekers, the outsiders, the broken and scarred folk, who turn up in our assemblies. We create deliberate contexts in which they may experience our hospitality, ask questions, and be allowed to look, taste, and see what we are all about. Many of the monastic orders have known this for centuries, but our churches rediscovered this "threshold ministry" which welcomes the friends who are strangers to everything we believe and stand for. Before these persons make any decisions, there is much they need to experience and learn in order to become part of the disciplines of our missional (and alternative) community. Our churches are intentionally and compassionately alert to the context of our evangelizing work. The church is formed to "seek and save" with utmost cultural and personal sensitivity and with biblical integrity.

SURPRISES

Though the older patterns, structures, and comfort zones began to disappear rather quickly at the turn of the century, it was not at all a negative experience. Questions about the integrity of the whole scene, which had smoldered under the surface for years, became insistent. The Spirit opened eyes, gave new vision and understanding, and energized folk to take seriously the reality that God was alive and well among his own. A new optimism and a new sense of the reality of the missionary confrontation produced an intensity of study, prayer, and obedience that were totally unexpected and hitherto unexperienced.

Life Out of Death

Anyone reading and thinking about the story of Saul of Tarsus will be aware that our God not only has a sense of humor, but also intrudes his grace in surprising (left-handed) ways in order to carry out his good purpose in the world. One wonders just who was out there, out of sight, praying for the powerful conversion of that persecutor of the church. Just so, as the cultural and ecclesiastical *diastrophism* took place around the Presbyterian Church, there were many, many patterns and structures that simply ceased to exist or wandered off into oblivion. At the same time, God was not absent. Quite the opposite. Surprises of grace. Some of the most articulate voices of unbelief and *death* inside the church became the "victims" of God's surprising and converting grace. Arrogant scoffers out of the academy were brought to tearful repentance. Proud leaders were brought to childlike faith, true humility, and new life in the Spirit (with manifestations that astounded their former colleagues).

This was also the case with some particular congregations which had been primary exhibits of ecclesiastical sterility, formality, and unbelief. Into those, most inexplicably, came outbreakings of life. Scriptures, formerly read with indifference, flamed with urgency and with power. Not only members but pastors and leaders became new creatures in Christ, i.e., they were powerfully converted and became champions of the gospel. Ah! There's nothing so wholesome as truly converted church leaders. Those watching from the outside simply could not explain it. But it was undeniable. God of wonders. The sovereign God is also the sovereign Spirit who creates the church. The kingdom of God does not just come in word but in demonstration of the Holy Spirit and power.

Rediscovery of the Gospel of the Dominion of God

Also in the midst of the chaos that took place back there at the turn of the century, the awakened (Reformed) community rediscovered its own theological heritage. For several decades prior to that time, churches from many traditions, primarily out of the "two-thirds world," had already been focusing on the New Testament theme of the "Gospel of the Kingdom (Dominion) of God." Their awareness of this theme's dominance in the gospel accounts also gave them a heartening awareness that the sovereign Lord was not absent in any of their daily, and often intractable, realities. It forced them to look deeply into the character of that kingdom and to realize that it radically redefined life, meaning, power, joy, . . . i.e., it redefined the totality of human experience. The Sermon on the Mount is clear testimony to this.

Our awakening men and women began to note that this is exactly what lies at the heart of our own (Reformed) understanding of the New Testament faith. It is interesting that this reminder and provocation came back to us from our Christian brothers and sisters from the other nations which had once been our mission fields. Those Christians, often living in the most distressing circumstances with power and joy, were practicing and living by this kingdom understanding all along. They saw, with New Testament eyes, that the sovereign God had come in Christ to inaugurate a true New Creation (another term for the kingdom of God). Forgiveness of sins and new life in Christ were one dimension of that kingdom, but it was much more wholistic than that. While North American Christians in the late twentieth century were marketing the gospel with all kinds of "self-fulfillment" gimmicks, and truncating expressions of the gospel, they had almost overlooked the fact that when Jesus came, he spoke of a kingdom, a new reality that was all-encompassing.

This New Creation would not define itself, or express itself, by any of the popular, economic, political, or power strategies or definitions of human design. The irresistibility of the kingdom defies human explanation. It comes as a subtle subversion. Its power and wisdom are "hidden" in weakness and foolishness. But it is surely real. Such rediscovery became the working heart of our awakened church's life and mission. It precipitated, and continues to precipitate, our excited and wondering adventure. No matter how alien, how dark, how hostile, or how seductive the context of our lives, . . . that is exactly where the Lord has given us our calling and incarnation. It is here that we are a people of joy and hope.

It's a funny thing that it took (Reformed) Christians so long to wake up to that which was at the very heart of its own transformational heritage. It was the insistence of Christians from the dynamic two-thirds world church that woke us up to that. The sovereign God is alive and at work in ways beyond our asking or thinking. Nothing is impossible with such a God. The gospel enterprise is always out of control.

Movements Co-opted by the (Reformed) Household

I predicted (in my blueprint) that the refounded (Reformed) household would be much more of a Spirit movement than it would be a denomination. It is not surprising that in a culture where information flows so freely that our awakened participants could hardly be expected to "hide their candle." Christian movements that appeared from out of nowhere were soon infiltrated by our own bright minds and flaming hearts. I think of a movement that sprung up twenty-five years ago called the Promise Keepers. It was a men's movement of enormous vitality. Huge numbers of our Presbyterian men were involved. As these men came alive to our (Reformed) *weltanschauung,* they soon realized that this was a gift that they needed to share—and did. It wasn't long before our awakened households became a major resource in giving content for that movement.

The same thing happened in most of the parachurch movements. The burning hearts and disciplined minds of our men and women became like the biblical leaven that leavened the whole loaf.

Symbiosis With Other Traditions

It is time to draw this retrospect to a close, but it needs to be said that another of our predictions about a post-denominational era has also been fulfilled. Our awakened households have benefited greatly by interaction with other traditions in this process. As our women and men rubbed shoulders daily with Wesleyans and Roman Catholics and Mennonites, they have come to appreciate some of the richness of those traditions and the historical stimuli that brought them into being. This was all brought back into our assemblies and processed in our growing awareness of our participation in the tapestry that is the larger "holy, catholic Church." But the reverse has also been true. As our folk realized that our (Reformed) heritage is not ours alone, but a biblical and theological understanding of transformational power, they freely shared it with their friends, so that assemblies of other traditions began to be enriched by our gifts to them as we have been by their gifts to us.

Not only so, but in this post-denominational era, we have found each other also in our mutual mission of being God's people of light in the midst of the darkness. We regularly share resources in our mutual love for each other, and especially in our mutual mission to obey Jesus Christ in the midst of the cultural darkness. It is good.

THE LAMENT FULFILLED, SO THE HOPE

It is very fulfilling to realize that what was such a scene of confusion, even lament, those twenty-five years ago has through the pain and the chaos become such a scene of life and hope. Particular forms of the church's life do, in fact, come to an end. Some are transformed into something quite different. Particular churches die, but *the Church* never dies. The living Lord is the one who is irresistibly building his Church. Nothing can or will prevail against him. Particular expressions of the mission of God (*missio dei*) can forget their calling and their reason for being called, but God is not thwarted by such unfaithfulness or forgetfulness.

So here we are in the year 2020, looking back. All we can do is celebrate the goodness and faithfulness of Jesus Christ, the Lamb of God. We can stand in awe before God's often strange and inscrutable ways which continue to triumph over the Beast in upside-down ways. We stand in worship that the Lamb is patient with our unbelief and our human foibles, and he allows us to share with him the pain and suffering that refine us and identify us more with himself. Jesus continues to walk among "the seven golden lampstands" which are his Church. He meets with his own people in their ongoing tribulations and fills them with his joy. Halleluia! We are witnesses!

Appendix A
The Fault Line and the Future

I do not intend to be melodramatic, nor do I think that I am. Yet it is a tragically dramatic moment within the life of the Presbyterian Church (U.S.A.) that will determine our future usefulness as a missionary community in the service of our Lord Jesus Christ. So what I intend to say here, I say very deliberately, knowing at the outset that some will hear but will not understand.

Occasionally we stand in front of a public map on a signboard, and a red dot on the map will indicate YOU ARE HERE. This essay is an attempt to identify where we are. The major debate in recent years over human sexuality and ordination standards has turned the lights on. What becomes obvious is that there is a fault line right through the PC(USA). The fault line is both epistemological (what is truth?) and Christological (who is Jesus Christ?). It is of such proportions that there is no possibility of a bridge. Even more dismaying is that those on opposite sides are not even speaking the same language, but rather talking right past one another.

It is all the more tragic because most Presbyterians don't understand such issues of philosophical and spiritual darkness and light. They are like the biblical sheep who follow whoever pertains to be their shepherd without discerning. It is difficult to relate biblical teachings about those teachers who will secretly bring in destructive errors (2 Peter 2:1) or those within the covenant community who are enemies of God insofar as the gospel is concerned (Rom. 11:28), with friends with whom we drink coffee and share the same ordination vows. Given our proclivity to be polite to everybody and to not give offense by such social improprieties, such a suggestion is even considered worse than heresy. So what has happened? Why such a dire description of the moment in which we stand?

It begins to dawn on us when we approach such an apparently biblical thesis that the ordained leadership of the church should lead exemplary lives (which has been assumed for centuries) only to be barraged with illusive language about "contextual interpretation" and about words that don't really have any meaning in themselves except with the meaning we invest in them. Oh? It reminds one of the line from Alice in Wonderland, "When I use a word it means exactly what I intend for it to mean. Nothing more, nothing less." It begins to dawn on us that our assumptions from scriptures and the confessional standards don't of themselves have any normative value to the church, which the church at the same time professes they do.

It begins to dawn upon us when a colleague in a theological school is ostracized for insisting that Jesus Christ is the divine Son of God as defined by the Council at Nicea. How does such come to pass in the schools that ostensibly are training men and women to be the pastors and teachers of God's people?

It begins to dawn upon us when we see the birthplace of the Reformation, which took these spiritual and intellectual turns generations before us, now a major mission field in the world, a veritable wasteland of spiritual darkness. How did that happen? How did we get to this place? What was it that Karl Barth saw seventy years ago so graphically that he suggested that the whole ecclesiastical scene was "demonic" which makes more and more sense to us today?

How did this venerable Presbyterian and Reformed body with its rich legacy of missions and theology get to the point where we no longer speak the same language within and where debate is not even possible? Here we are, a tradition which has affirmed that scriptures are not by private interpretation, but are the result of holy men speaking by the Holy Spirit, so that we have a sure word from God. We have exalted the need for theological education and for men and women to be skillful teachers of the Word of God, . . . only to find that the Word of God and the word of men are indistinguishable and in process of continual contextual change. How did all of this happen? Is there a blindness? Are we experiencing the reality of Luther's hymn?

. . . For still our ancient foe doth seek to work us woe
—his craft and power are great. . . .

THE BATTLE BEHIND THE BATTLE

First, it is important to reclaim the biblical principle that this present age is not neutral, i.e., that the "god of this world" is malignantly at work blinding, deceiving, and taking captive men and women morally, spiritually, and intellectually. The

Lamb and the Beast are at war. Wonderfully gifted, intellectually sophisticated, and socially charming people can be totally in the dark and can be clever (and effective) instruments of the darkness. It has always happened. It is happening. And it will happen.

This PC(USA) is built upon a solid assumption that God has spoken a clear word to his people. Of course it is spoken in different contexts. But it is unmistakable in whatever context. It is a word made flesh in Jesus Christ, and a word sealed with apostolic authority and the church's approbation for two millennia. Those who have joined the serpent-figure of Genesis 3 with the question, "Has God really said that?" have a track record through the centuries of exacerbating the darkness and leaving the world in the hopelessness of that darkness. Now we find that those foundational assumptions from scripture and the confessions are a strange language. We talk to each other but we do not hear each other. We are not on the same wavelength. There is something dark, even demonic, at work which challenges the integrity and authority of God's revelation.

A BIT OF HISTORICAL BACKGROUND

Our present battles are far more critical than these recent struggles would indicate. We have a virus in the system, and we need to track it. This is the same virus that Karl Barth saw in the 1920s. It is a virus that eviscerated the church's witness to Christ and to the Word of God. Barth indicated the virus was demonic in that it embraced principles from civilization and culture that denied the "otherness" of our Christian faith. It had come into the church primarily through the academy, through the universities and the theological schools. So with us.

The virus is traceable from contemporary figures such as Jacques Derrida, Michel Foucalt, and other postmoderns, who do slight-of-hand games with the use and meaning of words, back philosophically through Martin Heidegger at least to Nietzsche. But it has roots even before that in the whole Enlightenment project which exalted human reason above divine revelation. When the human subject and the human consciousness became the point of reference by which meaning, truth, and reality were determined, then, of course, scripture took on a marginal role. Because the culture had been so influenced by the Hebrew Christian tradition and the impact of scripture upon it, it was therefore given lip service and even studied. But the awe and mystery of having a somehow divinely energized communication that determined and formed and freed God's people became subservient to human agendas of the Enlightenment.

Please note that the church was embracing all of these self-contradictory assumptions within its womb. But as the church has moved into these recent decades, words have been determined to have no value in themselves, so that even as we study biblical texts, we invest the words with our own contextual meaning and so are able to cull out that which does not conform to the plausibility structures of our present neo-pagan society. Tragically, somehow this epistemic virus goes hand in hand with a reductionist view of Jesus Christ. More and more it is possible to have multitudes in the body of the Presbyterian Church (we are not alone) who are busy, who make decisions, who have lovely personalities, who are biblically indifferent, and who accept Jesus only as a significant human example, nothing more. Not Lord. Not Savior. Not Eternal Son of God. Not God of God, and Light of Light. Just a person of significance but not determinative of our life and salvation. Such marginalization of the authority of scripture as written has not only affected the normative role of scripture, but also that of our confessional interpreters.

For these past decades, we have walked together assuming we were all together with one heart and mind. We have had our family squabbles, but we knew that if we came together over scripture we could resolve them, forgive, and enter into new obedience. Oh, to be sure, there was a slight depression between us in the path that was getting deeper and wider, but we still had presbytery meetings, church night suppers, and endless coffee breaks together. But increasingly we found it difficult to talk across the chasm, now discerned to be a fault line. We seemed to speak a different language. It has been almost like Paul's awareness that communicating the gospel to unbelievers was not possible through human argument, only through the "foolishness of preaching."

The fault line betrays two subterranean tectonic plates. The fault line is the hardly visible meeting place of these plates. Yet these plates are of enormous consequence. On one plate are those children of the apostolic and evangelical faith that was heralded by the Reformation. That faith is periodically given fresh voice in the church's confessions. These children come out of different social and cultural contexts, but they are banners lifted to say to the world, "This is our faith and how it pertains to this culture and these crises. It is the faith of Calvin, Knox, Westminster, and of Barmen, and hence of our *Book of Confessions*." But on the other plate are those, who while sharing the same ecclesiastical household with the children of the Reformation, are children of the Enlightenment. While their theological language often seems the same, they begin with a different set of assumptions or presuppositions.

Tragically, there exists a huge company of vulnerable children who will follow whoever seems the most personable and convincing, either for good or ill. These are sheep who follow either a good or a false shepherd without discernment. They are easily led astray. Scriptures warn of this probability repititiously. What is difficult to grasp is that our fault line is between two mutually exclusive schools, and there is no common language and there are no bridges. We are on totally different grounds, with totally different presuppositions. And in our present confrontation over Amendment B, it is questionable whether real debate is even possible. On the surface it may all look the same, but it is not. And yet somehow we are friends and have long histories together, which makes it all the more painful.

This should not surprise any one of us either biblically or historically. The scriptures are replete with the issues of light and darkness, of truth and error, of Spirit and flesh. The subtlety which we face is that the aberrations of error come from within the community as "angels of light." The subtlety is that those who lead others astray are social friends. The question is always, How do we discern which is which? Historically it should not surprise anyone who has followed such comings and goings in the church over the last century. Such issues as the one now confronting us have long roots.

It should be apparent, especially to those who have followed the history of philosophical thought in the modern era. The fault is real and inescapable. It has to do with the epistemological question What is truth? and with the Christological question Who is Jesus Christ? Somehow, though different, they are the same. On one side of the fault line are the children of the Reformation with their biblical-confessional-missional focus (*Book of Order*, ch. 1, 2, 3). On the other side are the children of the Enlightenment, who in the church place their focus on the institution as a symbol of religious stability, and focus on polity (notice that the *Book of Order* gets fatter and fatter). The children of the Reformation have their roots deep in the theology of the confessions and the creeds, in their confidence that scriptures are uniquely of God, and their devotion to the Jesus Christ presented in those same scriptures. The church for them was, and is, a place where all of that was central as we engaged in our mission as given us by Jesus Christ, i.e. "the great ends of the church" (G–1.0200).

The children of the Enlightenment and of the modern era, on the other hand, had their roots deep in that focus on human reason and human autonomy. It was a movement which consigned "religion" to the private sector, with no respectable place in the academy. The movement focused on the human subject and relegated God and theology to the scrutiny and categories of human reason. Brilliant minds subtly disconnected themselves from (or were led astray from) a Christian-theistic epistemology (view of knowledge) and from the high Christology of the creeds. Theology was a human science and was conformable to endless *zeitgeists*. What this produced was Protestant Liberalism. More and more it began to take its prominent place as a subtle virus in the academy and in theological faculties.

The children of the Reformation and its scholars, being frequently ostra-cized from the faculties of schools dominated by Enlightenment philosophies, found their fulfillment in pastoral and missional careers. All of these took up habitation together within the Presbyterian Church. The children of the Enlightenment (who may not have even been aware that they had wandered onto another plate) progressively found their fulfillment in the church's institutional structures, as well as in its polity. The ideas of truth and error, orthodoxy and heterodoxy, and Spirit and flesh became increasingly unpopular—dismissable if not actually ridiculed. Such found no place in Enlightenment constructs.

As the optimism of the Enlightenment project with its structure began to crumble in the twentieth century, any connectedness with theological tradition also began to crumble. Thinkers such as Nietzsche attacked the whole modern concept of truth, and asserted that Western culture had separated itself from the transcendent. The whole postmodern era began to take shape. Another philosopher, Heidegger, took this even farther so that nothing, not even a word, has meaning in itself. His "view from nowhere" is the antithesis of Christian-theism. He asserted that our lives are a mystical experience that is neither objective nor subjective.

More recently, Nietzsche's true disciple Foucalt dismantled language even more by asserting that our human experience (and language) are socially and historically constituted—nothing more. Texts (such as scripture) have no single underlying structure and are infinitely complex. So a text can be a fascinating object of study, but it has no meaning in and of itself. Add to that the influence of Derrida who taught (too effectively) that language has no fixed meaning. Put this together and you have a kind of virus in the academy, and of course when it is in the academy, it also filters into theological faculties and thinking.

Watch how this surfaces in our recent constitutional struggles.

In the 1920s there was a brief moment when some Presbyterian scholars, children of the Reformation, sought to alert the church to the growing fault line inside the church between these Reformation and Enlightenment plates. Theological truth and error were made issues in a celebrated case. But when the children of the Reformation sought to force the issue (Gresham Machen and others), they were badly mauled on the basis of polity by the children of the Enlightenment, with their mastery of such. Since that time, these Reformation-evangelical folk in the Presbyterian family retreated to pastoral and missional roles primarily within congregations. This left governance essentially in the hands of the others.

Events intervened: the Great Depression, the Second World War, and the optimism of the 1950s. Then the postmodern virus began to show its face in popular culture. The 1960s produced all kinds of turmoil and radicalism and

"God-is-dead" theology. It is important to note here that for decades the training places for pastors had been a mixed bag, increasingly mirroring Enlightenment influences and decreasingly the biblical, Reformational, evangelical influences (these were never absent).

At the same time, we Presbyterians were in the same household. Still friends. We seemed to be unified but we were not. We all took the same ordination vows with reference to our faith in Jesus as Savior and Lord, as well as our acceptance of scripture and the confessions as norms for our life together. We assumed mutual sincerity. We seemed to be walking together, though as years went on the pathways diverged more and more. We all went to meetings of the General Assembly and affirmed our peace and unity. We differed, but then went out for coffee and laughed together as friends. But the subterranean plates were there, and the differences began to become obvious. The growing fault line is now impossible to bridge. And in the middle are still the innocent, trusting Presbyterian folk who follow their leaders like sheep, for good or ill.

Our present collision began in the 1970s when there came a push by an advocacy group to broaden our polity to an inclusive embrace for those of active homosexual behavior. There is a certain humorous irony in what happened. An unexpected response to a polity question came as a theological answer called "Definitive Guidance." The push, however, continued with a call for a study of human sexuality, and a controversial study ensued (mirroring all of the postmodern absence of absolutes), which essentially concluded that sexual norms were fluid in different cultural settings. Again, the General Assembly rejected the report and returned another theological answer— "Authoritative Guidance."

The advocacy continued to push the issue with a raft of overtures to open our polity to approve ordination for those of homosexual and lesbian practice. Again, a theological response came in the constitutional addition of G-6.0106 (b). What is interesting is that this amendment is essentially a confessional statement offered to interpret polity, which is precisely what the advocacy seeking to open the ordination process did not want. What the amendment says, in principle, is: "We believe . . . that ordination is not a right of polity, but rather the church's exclusive prerogative to affirm lives of repentance and faith, and of exemplary behavior according to the norms of scripture and of the confessions. This approval/ordination goes far beyond sexual behavior, and includes the total life under the Lordship of Christ." In short, theology determines polity, not vice versa.

Well, now, did that ever rip the cover off of the fault line. Now the two languages, the two subterranean assumptions, are graphically revealed. That theology should determine polity is unthinkable to the children of the

Enlightenment (even though they have vowed it in ordination). So the opponents of this principle used every major ploy to defeat it. One is from the legal profession and is called "reasonable doubt." Confuse the jury with all kinds of contradictory claims, and then say, "No law is better than a bad law." Just do nothing. What is sad about this is that the church and culture are crying for some clear word of guidance, and this proposes procrastinating even longer. It also infers that scriptures cannot help us here.

But more prominent is the ploy to marshal the scholars who use all of the linguistic sleight-of-hand principles of Heidegger, Foucalt, and Derrida, i.e., "a word has no meaning in itself" stuff. These opponents can on one hand exalt the text of scripture with all manner of wonderful scholarship, and on the other hand assert that it can only be interpreted in its own time and context, and cannot be normative for us in our new situation today. Say what? The bottom line is that scriptures are set aside as any understandable norm for life and faith.

So the two plates are simply (1) scriptures (and the confessions) are normative to determine faith and behavior, as well as the church's polity; or (2) malleable polity shall be normative to determine faith, behavior, and who is acceptable for ordination without reference to scripture and the confessions. All other arguments are but "smoke" to confuse. Both are choices. It is anyone's right to make such a choice, but we do it "in the presence of God and of Jesus Christ, who will judge the living and the dead, . . ." (2 Tim. 4:1).

Interestingly, our Reformed forebearer Karl Barth saw something of the same critical issue in Europe seventy years ago, and rang the figurative school bell in the playground of the theologians. Some heard. Some didn't.

Now it's our turn. When we cannot debate upon common ground and when our languages are different, then we simply confess. We employ the "foolishness of preaching." We pray for the eye-opening, life-giving Breath of God. That is an act of faith which believes that the same Spirit that energized the writing of scripture also works on our end to give us eyes and ears to receive a sure word from God. It is not silent here. God has spoken. Thus we children of the Reformation believe that it is altogether appropriate to place a clarifying theological statement in the polity to guide us in ordination. That's what theology is for.

We can proceed no further in our quest for a Presbyterian Church which is alive with the power of God to engage in its mission, and we certainly cannot enter the twenty-first century with any integrity as a community of the New Creation until we are refounded on our biblical, Reformational, confessional, and evangelical foundations.

Come Holy Spirit!

Appendix B
Suggested Further Reading

Anderson, Leith. *Dying For Change*. Minneapolis: Bethany House, 1990.

———. *A Church For the Twenty-first Century*. Minneapolis: Bethany House, 1992.

Ford, Kevin. *Jesus for a New Generation*. Downers Grove: InterVarsity, 1995.

Johnson, Ben. *95 Theses For The Church*. Decatur: CTS Press, 1995.

Leith, John. *Introduction To the Reformed Tradition*. Atlanta: John Knox, 1977.

Long, Jimmy. *Generating Hope: A Strategy for Reaching the Postmodern Generation*. Downers Grove: InterVarsity, 1997.

McGrath, Alister. *Evangelicalism and the Future of Christianity*. Downers Grove: InterVarsity Press, 1995.

Mead, Loren. *The Once and Future Church*. Bethesda: Alban Institute, 1991.

Newbigin, Lesslie. *Foolishness to the Greeks*. Grand Rapids: William B. Eerdmans Publishing, 1967.

———. *The Gospel in a Pluralist Society*. Grand Rapids: William B. Eerdmans Publishing, 1989.

Roxbugh, Alan. *Reaching a New Generation*. Downers Grove: InterVarsity, 1993.

Sine, Tom. *Wild Hope: Crises Facing the Human Community on the Threshold of the Twenty-first Century*. Waco: Word Publishing, 1991.

Snyder, Howard A. *Radical Renewal: The Problem of Wineskins Today*. Houston: Torch Publications, 1996.

Notes

Chapter 1

1. I acknowledge that there is that small but interesting group of folk whose whole identity is tied up in attending presbytery meetings, serving on committees, and being conscientiously involved in denominational busywork. They are a unique breed, and I honor their good intent. Having served on enough nominating committees, I also have grave questions as to the theological and missional credentials of many. Plus, I just don't happen to think that it has much to do with or is important to the mission of Christ. Forgive me if I am judgemental.

2. This Reformed tradition is succinctly stated in *Book of Order* (G–2.0500) as the particular flavor which we bring to the larger family of God. It is, of course, expressed in the several confessions contained in our constitutional *Book of Confessions*, as particular expressions of that Reformed understanding as the church coped with historical challenges in various cultural contexts. I will speak to it particularly in chapter 4 on the Majesty of the Sovereign God.

3. Daniel Yankelovich, *New Rules*, (New York, Bantam Books, 1982), xi ff.

4. A wonderful study of this impact is found in Abraham Kuyper's Stone Foundation Lectures given at Princeton Theological Seminary late in the last century, and printed under the title *Calvinism* and published by William B. Eerdmans in 1931. Kuyper was not only a theologian but also Prime Minister of the Netherlands, and therefore a product of the very Reformed tradition we are looking at here.

5. This is true, more than anyone will admit, even in our theological instutions which were established to insure that this very theological focus would not be obscured. Add to that the fact that our ordination proceedure has also not insured Reformed integrity. When the pastor-teachers are vague on this essential understanding, the chaos is exacerbated.

6. This is most evident at present in the "More Light" churches and those espousing the abandonment of biblical and confessional guidance in the ordination of gay and lesbian persons and others openly involved in lifestyles aberrant to God's design.

7. It would appear that it was out of just such a small group of students at the Sorbonne that John Calvin emerged into his role as bold spokesperson for reform.

8. Arbuckle's remarkable studies, primarily about Roman Catholic orders, are cogent and easily transferable into our current Presbyterian context, cf., *Out of Chaos* (New York, Paulist Press, 1988), and *Refounding the Church* (Marynoll, NY, Orbis Books, 1993).

9. I once, to my surprise, discovered a marvelously keen mind that was essentially Reformed on the staff of the Vatican in Rome and also teaching in one of the seminaries of the church.

10. See list of helpful studies at end of this volume.

11. In *Foolishness to the Greeks*, 144.

12. The present Southern Baptist "moderates" come to mind. These wonderful folk are frequently quite Reformed in their theological understanding. Baptismal differences are not of the essence of our theology (Karl Barth himself being a case in point).

13. One Christian journal carried a delightful account a few years ago entitled, "When the Bishops Went to Valdosta." It was the story of a Pentecostal congregation in south Georgia that discovered the beauty of the Episcopalian liturgies, and ultimately applied for membership in the Episcopal diocese. All the bishops in full regalia, shepherd's staffs and mitres, descended upon the congregation on a given day and were absolutely captivated by the combination of Pentecostal life and Episcopal liturgy. Why not?

14. I am more of an optimist than one denominational leader, who predicts that in thirty years there will not be more than six thousand congregations left!

15. From *Crossing the Postmodern Divide*, by Albert Borgman (The University of Chicago Press, 1992). Borgman is a primary source for further study into postmodernism.

16. Quoted in *PRISM*, 2 (February 1995).

17. To be honest, there were three or four workshop leaders and one platform speaker who were not Presbyterian and were invited for specific gifts they possessed.

18. A major study resource for those serious about this refounding process would be Richard Lovelace's *Dynamics of Spiritual Life* (Downers Grove, Ill.: InterVarsity Press, 1979).

Chapter 2

1. cf. Zephaniah 3:17

2. Dale Bruner gave a biblical exposition at the Presbyterian Congress on Renewal (1985), and spoke not of the prodigal son, but rather the parable of the prodigal father, who violated all sense of Jewish propriety by welcoming a son who had profaned the family name.

3. cf. Ephesians 3:21. Paul's prayer links the glory of God in the church and the glory of God in Jesus with the simple conjunctive "and."

4. I assume, with others, that this is a reference to the Holy Spirit, "the Spirit of glory and of God" of 1 Peter 4:14. cf. TDNT on δοξα.

5. Annie Dillard in *Teaching a Stone to Talk* (New York: Harper and Row, 1982), 40.

6. Romans 1:18.

7. Douglas Coupland, *Life After God* (New York: Pocket Books, 1994), 359.

8. The ancient heresy of Docetism denied the real humanity of Jesus, while affirming his deity. It is this making the Christian faith something of a denial of the incarnational realty of the faith for its adherents that has caused a resistance to come to grips with our real missionary confrontation with the world in which we live, with all of the ethical, communal, moral, and intellectual challenges of this reality.

9. Jacque Ellul has described this betrayal of the incarnation in *The Subversion of Christianity* (Grand Rapids, Mich.: William B. Eerdmans, 1986).

10. Lesslie Newbigin, *Foolishness to the Greeks* (Grand Rapids, Mich.: William B. Eerdmans, 1986), 132 ff.

11. Kurt Cobain and the rock group Nirvana are a telling evidence of an underground culture that caught everybody by surprise. The music industry thought they had the punk rock phenomenon all nicely packaged, deodorized, and controlled. From nowhere and without the hype and marketing of the industry, a voice of anger and despair came from Cobain and his group. They were almost instantly a hugely popular voice with their generation. When Cobain, himself a product of a broken home and tragic inner confusion, committed suicide, there was a huge wave of grief. When network news commentator Andy Rooney made disparaging remarks about Cobain, the network received an almost unparalled massive negative reaction to Rooney. It is an

evidence that most Boomers and their parents couldn't comprehend. But twenty-somethings did.

12. Did you ever notice that at the bookstore in the mall there are more New Age, occult, and Eastern Religion books than Christian? And did you ever watch who hangs around looking at those books?

13. While writing this, Ben Watterson announced the end of "Calvin and Hobbes" as a comic strip, and I am in grief.

14. Charles Mellis did a significant study of these in *Committed Communities: Fresh Streams for World Missions* (Pasadena, Calif.: William Carey Library, 1976). In the history of missions, it has been just such self-contained communities who have been able to move into difficult areas and become springs of Living Water.

15. Tim Dearborn, "Preparing New Leaders for the Church of the Future," *Transformation* 12:4 (Oct./Dec. 1995): 8.

16. See Ben Johnson's "Thesis #67" in *95 Theses for The Church*, (Decatur, Ga.: CTS Press, 1995).

17. Walker Percy has a fascinating book by this title in which he probes some of this lostness (as he does also in his novels), in dimensions that his psychiatric sensitivity picks up.

18. *Book of Order*, G–2.0500 b.

Chapter 3

1. The PC(USA) *Book of Order* begins with a clear focus on Christ as the reason for the church's existence. cf., G–1.0100.

2. This reminder of the uncontrollable and wild freedom of the Savior figure, Aslan, begins in the first of these chronicles when Lucy asks if Aslan isn't safe. "Safe?" said Mr. Beaver. "Don't you hear what Mrs. Beaver tells you? Who said anything about safe? 'Course he isn't safe. But he's good. He's the King, I tell you." *The Lion, the Witch and the Wardrobe* (New York: Macmillan, 1950), 75–76.

3. C. S. Lewis, *The Silver Chair* (New York: Collier Books, 1970), 157–58.

4. For an extended and most helpful study of the "upside down" concept, I recommend *The Upside-Down Kingdom*, by Donald Kraybill (Scottdale, Penn.: Herald Press, 1978) to whom I am indebted for my usage of this concept.

5. P. T. Forsyth, *The Soul of Prayer* (London: Independent Press, Ltd. 1954), 23.

6. Newbigin, *The Gospel in a Pluralist Society* (Grand Rapids, Mich.: William. B. Eerdmans, 1989), 228.

7. It is reminiscent of 1 Corinthians 1:27–30.

8. Mark Noll in *The Scandal of the Evangelical Mind* states that "the scandal of the evangelical mind is that there is not much of an evangelical mind" (Grand Rapids, Mich.: William B. Eerdmans, 1994), 3. Both he and Alister McGrath (*Evangelicalism and the Future of Christianity*) see the Reformed capacity for tough Christian thinking to be desperately needed in the whole of the evangelical movement and the church catholic as we face a non-congenial postmodern culture.

Chapter 4

1. *Book of Order*, G–2.0500.

2. cf., William Easum, *Sacred Cows Make Gourmet Burgers* (Nashville, Tenn.: Abington, 1995), 108 for a more thorough explanation of this as it relates to the church.

3. This hope was the *malkuth shemayim*, or the coming manifest reign of Yahweh, and was prevalent in the synagogues of post-exilic Israel.

4. This was nowhere more humorously true than in Martin Luther King, a prophetic voice whom few in the white Christian community could comprehend. When *Time* magazine wrote of him, it seemed to get the full irony of it all, explaining that King spoke to the white Christian South where they were most vulnerable, and where they least expected it, . . . he appealed to their biblical conscience!

5. I'm willing to use, also, descriptions such as extravagant, where-we're-not-looking-and least-expect, rambunctious, outrageous, sneaky, hilarious, surprising, and totally innovative—while acknowledging that these are all in the framework of God being faithful and true, sovereign and irresistible in love and grace.

6. Albert Borgman quoting Robert Bellah and others in *Crossing the Postmodern Divide* (Chicago: University of Chicago Press, 1992), 57.

7. Walker Percy, *Lost In The Cosmos: The Last Self-Help Book* (New York, Pocket Books, 1983), 7–8.

8. From an address by Robert Bellah at Fuller Theological Seminary, but also reflected in his conclusions in *Habits of the Heart*.

Chapter 5

1. Again, cultural anthropologist Gerald Arbuckle's point pertains here; when any [order/denomination] forgets, or displaces, or dilutes its *founding myth* (the beliefs, values, mission around which it was formed), then the order becomes *chaos*. With our points of consensus so shadowy in the mind of the Presbyterian Church, this is an accurate description of where we are.

2. Sadly, these institutions have, for the most part, become so conformed to the reigning cultural plausibility structures, that students come out wearing their "pious agnosticism" like a badge of honor along with their academic pride, yet less evangelized and more uncertain about the mission of God in Christ.

3. This reference to Isaiah 24:10-11 is a translation from the Hebrew by J. A. Motyer *The Prophecy of Isaiah* (Downers Grove, Ill.: Inter Varsity Press, 1993), 201–2.

4. Or, "What does all of this have to do with *Book of Order* on the Great Ends of the Church, the Church and its Confessions, or the Church and its Mission?" Or what does it have to do with Jesus' mandate and mission given to those whom he calls?

5. Barth puts it this way: "*But now* directs our attention to time beyond time, to space which has no locality, to impossible possibility, to the gospel of transformation, to the immanent coming of the kingdom of God, to affirmation in negation, to salvation in the world, to acquittal in condemnation, to eternity in time, to life in death—*I saw a new heaven and a new earth: for the first heaven and the first earth are passed away.* This is the Word of God." (*Epistle to the Romans*, Oxford University Press, 1980), 92.

6. *Book of Order*, G-2.0500

7. This is taken from Ken Medema's song "Is There a Place for Dreaming," from his album *Kingdom in the Streets* (Waco, Tex.: Word Inc., 1980).

Chapter 6

1. From a motto, which said in essence, "The church reforming and ever being reformed according to scripture."

2. One disclaimer needs to be entered at this point, and that is the unknowns of God's *providence*. We Reformed Christians believe that God is full of surprises, as well as being faithful to his own nature and good purpose in Christ. This very dramatic collapse of the modern era is probably one of those providences.

3. My mentor, Cornelius Van Til, described such a culture in the graphic metaphor of a "boundless, bottomless sea of chance."

4. By 2020 we can realistically anticipate that local and national governments will be much more restrictive in granting tax deductibility both toward church property and church contributions.

5. For instance, the idea of a Presbyterian Church wedded to its Scottish roots, what with the "kirking o' the tartans" and all such nostalgia, will have become utterly ridiculous.

6. I have often humorously, but honestly, said that my ideal Christian would be an amalgam of (a) the Dutch Calvinist's tough-minded Christian-theism; (b) the Pentecostal's sense of the present and dynamic power of the Holy Spirit; (c) the Mennonite's wariness of the seductiveness and tentacles of this present age; and (d) the Roman Catholic and Orthdox's sense of the mystery of church and sacrament. Not a bad mix.

7. This from the Creed of Nicea (325 AD).

Chapter 7

1. See *Book of Order* G–1.0200.

2. David Bosch quoting Martin Kähler in *Transforming Mission*, (Maryknoll, N.Y.: Orbis Books, 1991), 16.

3. The overwhelming theme in the synoptic gospels is that the Messianic Kingdom is now inaugurated in the presence of Jesus. It is preached as "the joyous news of the kingdom." In other New Testament writings it is variously expressed in the near synonymous concepts, such as Eternal Life, New Creation, Salvation, or Righteousness.

4. See Mark 1:14–15; Col. 1:13–14; Eph. 2:1–10.

5. cf. Bosch in *Transforming Mission*, 50 ff., in which he points out the ways in which the early church failed.

6. I hasten to state that there may have been good reason for this, since they had the immediate task of reclaiming the apostolic faith within the church. It is also interesting that Calvin apparently wrote the *Institutes* to equip the laity (in France) for their role as agents of Christian faith in their daily world.

7. In the early post-apostolic centuries, the field of apologetics was primarily to discern how the Christian faith engaged and presented its gospel to the pagan world. But when the missional focus was lost, a field of *polemics* was developed in which Christians of different persuasions engaged one another. In the process, the world outside of the church, that world of real lost men and women, became obscured to far too much of the church.

8. See John Leith, *An Introduction to Reformed Tradition* (Atlanta, Ga.: John Knox Press, 1978), 100 ff.

9. One would do well to read Gordon Fee's *Paul, the Spirit, and the People of God* (Peabody, Mass.: Hendrickson Publishers, 1996). Fee does a superb job of exegeting Paul's great emphasis on the life of the Spirit in the Christian community.

10. See *Book of Order* G–2.0500 (1).

11. cf., also *Book of Order* (G–5.0000). This passage indicates that such an idea is very much understood in our polity. The only problem is that no one has bothered to communicate this covenant to the membership of the Presbyterian Church.

12. Leith, *Introduction to the Reformed Tradition*, 71ff. *Book of Order* G–2.0500 (4).

13. *Book of Order* G–2.0500 (2), and G–3.000.

14. Also seminaries can become irrelevant. I speak as an ordained pastor-teacher and have often been accused of being too hard on clergy. But my very real "lover's quarrel" with seminaries is that while the idea of well-equipped teachers is valid, even necessary, too often the whole process is abstracted from the missional design of the church and its offices and the proven gifts of the Spirit.

15. Mark Noll, *The Scandal of the Evangelical Mind* (Grand Rapids, Mich.: William B. Eerdmans, 1994), 3.

16. Leith, 77ff.

17. Newbigin, *The Gospel in a Pluralist Society* (Grand Rapids, Mich.: William B. Eerdmans, 1989), 229.

18. G–2.500 (3), but perhaps most cogently stated in Lesslie Newbigin, *Gospel In A Pluralist Society* in which he spells out (as a Reformed missiologist) what it is going to mean to be the church in a postmodern culture.

Chapter 8

1. In chapters 2–4 we looked at "Mission: Where the Darkness Is the Greatest," "Sheer Devotion to Christ," and "Sovereignty: An Absolute and Not an Abstraction." Hence, a focus on mission, on Christ, and the Sovereignty of God.

2. *Book of Order*, (G–2.0500).

3. According to Alister McGrath, there is no existing evidence that John Calvin was ever ordained. *A Life of John Calvin*, (Grand Rapids, Mich.: Baker Books, 1990), 97.

About the Author

ROBERT THORNTON HENDERSON GREW UP IN WEST PALM BEACH, Florida. He graduated from Davidson College and Columbia Theological Seminary, with special studies in apologetics at Westminster Theological Seminary. For forty years he pastored congregations in North Carolina and Louisiana, primarily in university settings. He was denominational staff person in the field of evangelism for the Presbyterian Church in the United States (PCUS) from 1975 through 1979, and he has written extensively about evangelism and congregational renewal.

For the past seven years Henderson has served as Director of Seminary Ministry for Presbyterians for Renewal. He is also associate editor of CATALYST, a journal for seminarians, which keeps him in contact with congregations across the nation as well as students and faculty in eighteen seminaries. He currently lives in Tucker, Georgia, with his wife, Betty Colburn Henderson. They have four children and four grandchildren.